this is the summoning to return to the way of nigga ways back to the nigga way an attempt at liberating the space place in yo head now occupied territory yet these apocalyptic werds mite settle git in where they fit in n persuade metamorphosis along a new path of resistant behavior whereas i an indigenous NAKED NIGGA is hoo i been hoo i embraced hoo NIGGA is a way of being thinking and seeing living period hoo you are hoo i am that i am hoo all real niggaz wheresumever they wee may bee are is tis when aint that a bitch realization hit me and i knew i came out seemingly b4 mah time to this muthafuckin earth not mah fault as frum a dimensionless thought of thought seed yah I was an organism expanding mah will cuz nothing kan stop a nigga who time has cum to be placed down as far back as i was able to be and as i flowed out mah daddy dick in the deepest fornix part of mama pussy in a napolean creole southern ghetto trap town hyped hoodoo hood hooded secret society type situation that spit mee out wit a mission not determined by me for one reason or anutha hoo was presented dishonorably wit left over sin to walk amongst mah peeple since time had cum for the Way of Nigga Ways In The Year of Our Lord The White Man per according to a JEWISH Calendar aye hoo misappropriated okay STOLEN our culture dating naming and saying exactly when shit happened and when shit aint happened even tho they Jews bka plain old Caucasoids said thus and thus I came into the slippery labian folds of the desolate city opioid suburbs crooked counties corona dreams covid coercions uh in the belly of back black alleys a NIGGA is born butt a few days and he full of trubbles on the dubble limited ambitions n misery ready to chew him up whereas yo family that U were born wit is not to be the family that you bond wit how kan U Be Born into a Family that immediately sees you as the enemy huh when all u did was show up unwanted apparently as he hoo came forth in these beginnings like a rose flower growing frum concrete niggaz are all co-experiencing the exact same thang at the exact same time not because we live in parallel universes butt becuz we Live in parallel hoods ya digg we all dying living & being born at the simultaneously time like roaches and other Vermin in hoods that we learn to stand up for cuz we think its good butt standing up for the HOOD never seems to lead to anythang good we dont own the concrete that the street is made frum is that our fault or does the fault lie wit the stars still we FIGHTIN over concrete that we will die upon after 5-0 shoots us down with our hands in the air or we kill each other based on rumors then out cum the teddy bears bearing witness hoo cares & strange black folk marching aint got no army protesting on yo behalf butt not wile you U were alive paying bills whereas it dawned on mee there was no bevy of beauties in this dense universe like I

THE NAKED SOUL OF A NIGGA

by
Reverend Nigga Daddy

Copyright: 2020
Publisher: Real Nigga Publishing
All rights reserved. No part of this book may be reproduced or transmitted in any form or by any means without written or permission from the author.

This book is dedicated to all Real Niggaz everywhere round Da World. And In YO Neighborhood.

seent on the commercial that tole me I cood be sumbody if I was good-looking enuff which U cant be when U hungry wit no change of drawls for a indeterminable length of time U just kno U smell like hell theres funk then theres funky then theres rotten summa-ma-bitch then theres CaDaVeRous muthafucka often no recovery or respite for quite-a-bit in sum cases at least without soap and water part of yo medikal industrial complex health plan but U didnt plan to B so U didnt have a plan A or B urged by Brotha CHESTER HIMES wit a pistol as antidote for what ails a nigga when him see substance aint illusion its often delusion and an attempt to induce separation frum matter only leading to alienation emptiness butt now you pick up on what happens to the best of us when u lurch fall frum yo perch got you in search of meaning self SOMETHING of substance abuse rules ya mind tho the bottle keeps ya warm on cold nites cuz the spirits that reside in the genie of the bottle been better to U than GOD been to most muthafuckaz hoo worship after voracious readings of scripture this inspite of wind chill n pills they want u to take Uncle Sam took U out his WILL cuz U Served rongly rather than strongly as is the line in the sand U shall not cross TRUE you a Vet butt treated like a Dog so yo doctor a Octogenarian Veternarian wit memory loss give YOU a shot and HIMSELF too in ya hindleg after lying down wit dogs u git up wit Please and Thank U lemme ast U sumpen U ever been disappointed not in what you ARE butt in what U mite have been when U think it all the way out dejected bout the future that never arose due to yo present at the time now past at the moment yet still yo will desires understands what cood be n that shit affect you for worse like-a-relationship sanctioned by the church putt it like this you make the mooves that will git U ahead be not duped beheaded butt fall for the okey doke frum a Nigga U thawt U knew butt didnt U only thawt U did cuz he gave U artificial intelligence the I have a dream speach manipulating n managing you into a false construction so u fell for the milieu of possibilities theories equations postulates hypotheses designed to lead u into madness butt boff him and Martin were traitors to separation U aint see dat tho til it was too late til u were chasing a neverending storied solution a riddle that does not exist only the question derived frum a false premise in the first place yo void volume space unfulfilled unassured denied innerstanding now u living outside the apartment u paid good money for and caint fuck the white girl wit the bad teef n tiny dog no mo that nobody else wanted she fed ya stripped down ego so u succumbed to a has been had by the hood denizens dastardly decadents hoo set a precedent in how they fucked her before yo dick even knew she existed n stood in line in yo hand U gotta face facks face destiny accept a losers dismemberment a fools initiation a bath in vomit a life of desperation U was set up like the sun held in high esteem a minute then got big in the head the moon timed yo exit the sky watched u leave yo pride under the door mat wit the key no longer welcum to eavesdrop on ya roommate fucking a pig U jack off to reciting an important mantra old testament prayer butt U aint kno U was dealing wit HOES of the Tribe hoo whudden on yo Vibe unh when u gone unnerstand dat er body dat LOOK like You aint YO peeple traitors cum in all races places spaces cases to brang U down like dem twin towers on judgement day cuz thats what dat shit was not for Niggaz per se butt for Amerikkka The BRUTEtiful Whereas the ratio so many of Us are WALKING around with the GHOSTS of DEAD white men stuck fathoms leagues deep in our DOMES our synpatic stimulie messy nervous systems confused consciousness the vilest violations as guiding mythos whether its JESUS or MUHAMMAD and increasingly even BUDDHA for the mo sophisticated negroid fooled again believing the white man a SPIRITUAL LIBERAL instead of the RAVENOUS WOLVES he actually is hiding under Cloak of AFRA ASCENDANT nature cums PRAYS with Us lowly blacks then PREYS slowly on U.S. lowly blacks while we KNEELING wit our not fully consecrated HANDS or FISTS in the Air KNEELING for a FEELING jack while we suffer Attacks Slings Arrows outrageous misfortune BULLETS that the United States manufactures wholesale wit Niggaz NAMES already on em dipped in IRONY and FATALISM so that they wind up in our melanated BACKS in yet another

Anonymous SINnonymous Hood from Cops who said they FEARED for their lives even tho they are the only one who had a GUN when its all said done Son Cops aint under no STATUTE of LIMITATIONS wee just Burdened wit LAMENTATIONS from the myriad DIRGES we BEholding wee gotta avoid equality religious dogma n seek balance instead so to use the Tools of LOGICK REASONING to Inspect ASSERTIONS that APPEAR To Be TRUTH butt AINT For Us wee are KONTROLLED frum the WOMB to the TOMB Frum the CRADLE to the grave taught to behave identically by attitudes of magnitude by the likes of racist Santa KKKlaus who calculate our Lifespans for when wee good or badd and put that shit sumwhere in a Chart for future reference at the North Pole AFTER Him and his peeples determine how much Money they kan make off Us DEAD or ALIVE dat aint no jive Niggaz are just CARCASSES to throw on a Heap We have donated our Bodies to science while we are Yet n still walking around IN them Wee be Barometers against which MR CHARLEY gauges His PROFITS lassoed willy nilly into silly DOCILITY via the CHURCH Whiteys Chicken Wang PREACHERS who sell us Heaven while the GROUND is STOLEN frum up under U.S. for the Great BY and BY in the uncurved SKY awaits us brothaz n sistaz when we CRY and DIE or we long for our Soul to be made whole and go back to hollywood swangin frum sum trees plains monkeys in Edgar Rice Burroughs Tarzan-Kontrolled AFRIKA as Freaks frum whence we NEVER came anyway Once they passed the CIVIL RITES ACT white folks aint ACTED RIGHT since meanwhile niggaz caught AIDS n the rainbow colored prideful destructive Monkey choked from the Federal Aid they gave Niggaz that was tainted swathed swarmed sworned scorned Cops in thecity arresting u while Pedophilia n Perversion goes unchecked in the Suburbs white trash trailer parks go unnoticed by 5-0 They give Niggaz WATER and tell em not to SPIT on the sidewalks tho always holding us to a higher standard of depravity that gits them elected to politcal orifice offices while black men women git locked up for less than PINCHING-a-Muthafucka in this Behavior Modification Concentration Camp called Amerikkka sadder is the unfortunate muthafuckin FACK Jack that so many of our own Sistaz and Brothaz are these COPS that wont STOP their shit that they are involved in doing to Us The WHITE MAN is still the DEVIL butt werse is now the BLACK MAN is The DEVILS HELPER the Evolution of Virginia Slim CIGARETTES have cum further than pigmented masses have ya digg as they represent White Womens Metoo Libgtq in being FREE in Society U woulda THUN:K that woulda been about the Progress of Black Folks Amerikkka is built on a fake fraud broad called history which is actually a mystery a delishis curiosity no form of Divine Enlightenment cums available to most of us until its way past our bedtime like Water seeks its own level the Mind seeks its Own Truth and if u wait long enuff the Lie will reveal itself for and its PERPETRATORS VICTIMS BELIEVERS the story of the awakened nigga begins with PERCEPTION of Real Truth cums outta niggaz loins turn on tune in to yo inner divine nigga figga our environs quickened back to the body wrapped in skins the sickened heightened back to normalcy wee repopulate as a mandate in place our animist desires will be carried forth for this is the spark of nigga life many of us hoo travel alone singular in life and its betta dat way being able to go faster further by yo lonesome without the werrisome the single mindedness is the essence of the one nigga moovement n groovement the me myself I the you yo self n u mooving solo dolo in silence n violence where necessary real niggaz form alliances over friendships relationships butt only wit those of the highest nigga caliber testing all allies by da amount of real nigganess they possess trying the spirit by the spirit n try the a nigga by a nigga real nigga mandates must always bee in place in the space hoo ever u face neva sced to embrace their niggahood or da werd nigga the figga inside em the evolving TRAITS a better way to kno thought frum thinking realms and not until then when synchronicity konnects can anythang like REALNESS re-attainment revelation enter his Being ya digg the holes in a Nigga have got to be filled wit sumpen and most time its FAKE FILLINGS leading to Fake FEELINGS primitive loins longing for sumpen idolizing much he dont even know bout on a deeper shadow authorized level cuz he or she dont kno how to moove apart frum society so dependent on Crackaz so average negroids go along n bee a machine that whitey pulls the plug or turns the switch off on em just going along to git along is how most of us Niggaz operate to date Shit we ALIENS on our own planet facing uncouth untruths EXTERRESTRIAL NIGGAZ waiting on the MOTHERSHIP along with DR YORK and the HONORABLE ELIJAH MUHAMMAD Or look for that shit in the WHIRLWIND like MARCUS GARVEY tole us to do cuz he was cumming back life a thief in the nite frum the abyss on sum BLACK JESUS vibe tribe not sum disembodied voice offering the self pity titty and we knoweth that shit not as the elites kno butt as everythang we ARE and KAN Be is writ quotidian quantitatively large inside the skin of a Nigga as part of our DNA aka Divine Nigga Attributes we gotta brang to the daylite of our existence that is yet unseenable yah butt the BELIEF is Quicker than the KNOW in this Muthafucka and it gits to our way of Understanding before anythang else We BLESSED and BLISSED with da Shizz Too much Belief and and not enuff KNOW Mah Daddy useta tell me shit like this smelling like TOBACCO and Black Leather Coat that he wore And I wood fall asleep under his arm while he droned on drilling drops of slop as ammunition as nutrition for attrition into mah head that I wood have a chance to VALIDATE once once they sprouted in mah veins reached manhood mah NUTS dropped like low hangin fruit signs a nigga mind was ripe and ready to receive further reproof instruction other than more than LIES Whitey had taught me to Acknowledge VERIFY and VALIDATE is sum important shit else U go thru life being PISSED ON and tole its just RAIN, heahme And hoo wanna live a life such as that I dont believe in the SANCTITY of the HYMEN of a HOE aint only RONG its UN-CIVILIZED Its like trusting in Whiteys Hypothesis of Pscience tho it be False and built upon a STUDIED OPINION passed off as FACT then TAUGHT to the UN-SUSPECTING Gullible Ig-nant Niggaz So we done wind up accepting Science that even tho it DENIES the SENSES makes Sense cuz a lotta times they give it to us warped wrapped up in a MATHEMATKAL REPOSITORY Thus Cracker PSCIENCE has Taught us how to DISTRUST Our very own Senses as Nonsenses depending instead on WHIMS of THEM Writing THEORIES long into the Nite by Candlelight and (nowadays) Fluorescent Lightbulbs Never to emerge from their Ivory Towers or Halls of Academia into the Real world For the Residence of E-Vil that is Pscience has become the PROVINCE of MINDS bent on EMBELLISHING The TRUTH rather than PROOVING That the TRUTH EXISTS (I THINK THEREFORE I AM aint shit) by TOUCHING, SEEING, HEARING, FEELING, TASTING n THINKING TRUTH is at such a Minimum in this Muthafucka that People have becum more in The MOOD For FALSIFICATION and MANIPULATION of Their CONSCIOUSNESS And MOTE It Be and SO It T-I-Tis This is where we BE at a Niggaz time in OUR-story of HIStory The WAR is for Every Nigga VERY Mind for us to figger out the consequence of being conquered consistently by punk rulers tho bowed unbroken non-stagnant a frustrated mankind true yet Niggaz still got an imperative form of giant significance we just dont be marching no mo in them skreets so Yo eyes SCANNED by the NSA who thats all they doing when Niggaz Gather in CROWDS is Patrolling and Kontrolling our RETINAS to feed a DATABASE of Niggaz they keep underground sum muthafuckin where prolly in New Yawk--and maintained by The PRISONER Pop they be giving jobs calling Yo house as Debt Collectors aint THAT sum shit Niggaz still going to The Penitentiary to git a JOB since he UN-EDUcATED rite a nigga hoo done gone to skool for 12-25 YEARS is just as INSTITUTIONALIZED as a Nigga hoo been LOCKED UP for 12-25 Years Cumming out of The Joint a 75% mauled gnarled Hueman to a deconstructed society that has mooved on frum U and onto sumpen Un-recognizable or Cognitive to even the best of us forgit the rest of us you make attempts to rebalance to become sumpen akin to the Nigga you once was before U defiled yo self u played yo self caint blame nobody else knowhatimean butt now u in the time where u mah nigga must cum back to yo highest nigga self that u becum not just a free nigga butt a free Thinking nigga figga Life being what it is and what it aint makes the difference in how a lotta Muthafuckaz succeed against the ODDS set by AMERIKKKA wit its CASINO POLITRICKS and hoo wants Niggaz to respeck the White Mans inevitable hate cheat spiraled outta kontrol at the dawn of his savagelization for Us skeduled to go to eternity endless infinity we been placed indiscriminately disproportionately into a shituation not of our doing in these latest episodes of depopulation agenda by the united snakes of amerikkka so we wont rise above 13% of the hate for us how is it a Man is PaRoLed by the STATE butt GOD and You caint see eye to on a GOD-dam thang like you EVER did tho fo real Please note this aint a PREACHING Manifesto this-a-REACHING manifesto using genderless werds tryna reach unreachable niggaz made frum manna man on the skrimf of the kinds of hood-o-rama drama we all done cum thru not Un-scathed butt dam sho unbowed by integration n stimulus checks for the wretchedness that surrounds bounds us due to martin luther kings talented 10th sellout aesthetics therefore even the green dollars dont live in da black hoods no mo the level of exploitation sexploitation debasement knows no end in site aight dont forgit dred Scott tole u dat shit in the city of Saint Louis where aint no saints and to this day whiteys laws reflect his innermostest thawts for stopping cock blocking the advancements of the duly put upon nigga chances we mo than a nuisance to the beast of revelation we are a bonafide sertified publick enemy threat to his existence in his mind while he robbing da hood of all its good for leaving it destitute n deplorable warning when ya dump all yo emotions into that feeding period of misspent youth thinking u cood do no wrong cuz U was strong and full of wet cum now yo shit dried up U so U shooting 2by4 dust and the world belongs to the likes of young niggaz U aint never seent afore a lotta them different now born of PRE-CUM instead of the FULL NUT so they BITCH-NIGGAZ sumpen that caint be explained in the Medical Diagnostic Manual despite the fack that much of what passes for MEDISIN is based on the DISMEMBERMENT disembodied classroom study of niggaz FOR SALE to the Highest Bidder coons negroids are born n made manifesting traits symptoms about their lipps eyes hearts MONSANTO GLAXO SMITH KLINE MERCK ABBOT Microsoft love to use propaganda to beat truth declaring perpetuating long trains of tyrannies insoluble atrocities novel oppressions announcing niggaz burials so many of us go round wit filled wit rong hostilities for the rong Inner Me rather than the Barbarians at the Gate summa our minds burn way down wit self hate ZORA NEALE HURSTON measured Niggaz foreheads and tole U that by extension the work the Gubmint long been involved in using nigga Men as MULES n GUINEA PIGS & TEXTBOOK measuring our emotions calling the final hurt an accident when ever we stiffened and our minds inhibited itself and we woke irrationalized or cowered examples abound just ask HENRIETTA LACKS jack for facks all U gotta do is take a Rocket to the Moon that they cant show U how they got THERE WHERE they left her GENETIC MATERIAL on summa dem Regolithic Rocks so they say cuz I aint telling U what I heard Im telling U what I been RUMORED to know n understand about THE MAN and how his MIND BEHIND da scene werks when nobody looking and they Cooking the phallic-driven history books to keep us shook seeing as how PERCEIVED VALUE is Greater than INTRINSIC VALUE or actual factual value as the case may be know full well that every thang that GLITTER aint GOLD or shouldnt be SOLD as such like when JAMES BALDWIN yelled fire next time down a crowded memory lane and niggaz rushed for the exit still its true a nigga shouldnt hide his LITE under a Bushel but that it SHINE so All Niggaz kan see it from a far distance especially them Niggaz lost in the Wilderness of an Increasing Gentrified yet uncivilized Amerikkka LADY LIBERTY not withstanding cuz she aint shining Her lite for Niggaz she aint wanting Niggaz to stop Tossing and Turning and being Tired yearning to be FREE See thems Empty words and Niggaz is the one who MADE the Muthafuckin STATUE now the Bitch sits on the JURY when niggaz go to trial for sumpen he aint doo She mo like a STAUTE of LAW against the very Nigga ideals embedded into it we shooda raped her when we had the chance aye NO we aint gone surrender our compass consciousness those hoo kno and refuse to rot to the core wee gone scrape to the end as niggacestors made outta southern unreported rebellions did doo down to the white meat fast twitch sinew cuz wee as the peeple peeple of the soil wit awareness n emotion bee cognizant of at sum level our descent frum wuthering heights fall frum our glory story yet we have an ADAPTIVE MOLECULAR STRUCTURE as all Niggaz MUST hoo aint inert as old as we are in Earth years so dont trip to git torn miserably aye because EVERY THANG is FLEETING and was Never Yours in the way that The CRACKA claims shit Uggh the only thang that BELONGS To You is YO SELF and thats where U shood Pour most of Yo muthafuckin INNERGY taking KARE of Yo Self LOVING Yo Self RESPECTING Yo Self HONORING Yo Self ya heahme and not allowing other Muthafuckaz to cross or disrupt dem BOUNDARIES to DISRESPECK dem Boundaries cuz deep inside U Born with knowing Whats Yours is Yours and it will always cum back to you no matter what in sum shape form or fashion butt that which you CANT Own and SHOULDNT own you Will NEVER own this gnosis is in you like SCRIPTURE cuz we are the history the very lining of all that is we aint gotta study to be show ourselves approved since we the repository depository crackaz sced thats why the blood shed so blood will be spared for niggaz tho as we go on being round and is read and thunk by you when U pay attention see Amerikkka is a bankrupt bizness cartel west indies charter massachusetts corporation that we dont allow ourselves to git caught up in as ruthless Capitalist Niggaz wit no home training git Yo money without losing site of the fact that WALLSTREET while started on the Wet Backs and Bloodstreams of niggaz shouldnt be allowed to consume ya principles of Cooperative Economics one unto another thats that UBUNTU afrikan amerikan turtle island shit we all fall down 2gether and RISE too OR we dont Rise at all frum the ashes or dust to dust of course many of Our folk fucked themselves up reading KARL MARX tom bout eaching according to NEEDS n Niggaz thawt dat made sense butt aint kno Marx whudden tom bout OUR black asses since he hated Niggaz just on the skrimf of pure economic hypocrisy philosophy be that as it may many of us will dance to the music of our treasonable unreasonable endemic enemies and kill ourselves on their behalf destroy whole wholesome hoods in the service of Uncle Sammy baby then claim blackness when UNK turns on em like JUDAS now we wanna cum back HOME where We USETA Beelong until we became long gone TRAITOROUS Souljahs u know dem Kind dat SPIT on they own dat ack as da DOGS they are when fraudulent greedy degenerate Unk SIC em on U.S. weaponless and defenseless cuz we PRAYING and TRAITOR JOE is PREYING for Him BOSS on HIS Peeple cuz 4 sum strange reason Martyric Niggaz like lay dying after being own up while they Talking to

God about the WHITE MEN who aint gone never be labeled as TERRORISTS altho they SHOOD Be but aint cuz it aint WRITTEN yet it ain't GITTING No easier to deny the TRUTH That WHITE FOLKS are TERRORISTS even LYNCHING LAWS cant HANG wit em when it cums to the Shit they do under cover of burning hoods psychological parades in the LIGHT Yet Niggaz KNEELING and not BREATHING putting they HANDS UP KISSING ASS VOTING Going to SKOOL gitting EDUCATED and GRADUATED merry like christmas buying spending binging making WHITEY RICH and STILL Wee DIE many wit suffcent cowardice without a WILL to LIVE thats recognized anyWHERE in da LAND that wee hold the DEED To within STAMPED without on Our SKIN as ALLODIAL TITLE in a MANOR we Born to butt THEY Jealous OF so FOUL STENCH ILL-ROTTEN GAINS Plague our existence to be merely a CHOSEN Simple Peeple of NO HARM SO MEEK yet why is This WEAK in the Eyes of those who desire our DEMISE the WISE Whisper our SALVATION because wee HEAR Differently in the same Space that Crackaz have Conquered via FAA Frequencies wee not Own since it costs $5G Kan U digg it as I TRY Caint CRY no mo to git U 2 C SUMPEN about a PHENOMENON call it a SPECTRE a Cloud used by SORCERERS, MEDIA to make sumthing exist that is Not yet used to EXTINGUISH a Peeple like U.S. Aint even a SECRET No Mo the SYMBOLISM by itself tells as it Sells and Niggaz grow HUNGRY for a PROTEST sponsored by

The USUAL SUSPECTS whose LIVES MATTER as long as there is a PROFIT at the End of the LGBTQIA RAINBOW HOE-A-LITION them so BLACK n PROUD they say it LOUD and rip off JAMES BROWN But that was BLACK when BLACK Men n Women had clearly defined ROLES and the POWER STRUGGLE was against MITEY WHITEY less against fermented crispr microbes now Wee Conquered & Divided Undecided WHO is Who frum the Boys frum the Girls frum the BITCHES to The BITCH-NIGGAZ and We Blame it on The WATER maybe its the MSG in the SOY SAUCE Butt U ever notice that Aint No Country a Country that dont have its WOMEN under KONTROL which is why NIGGAZ aint got NO Country Hell we aint got no HOMES either in which a Black Man is HEAD of the HOUSE 80% of the time Nigga aint got No CASTLE he aint gone have No Country neither A Nigga hoo caint Stand His Ground caint stand his self Our Wommin and Men do exist EXCEPT most of Males and Females BITCHES and HOES or BITCH NIGGAZ the FAULT for that ain't in the STARS cuz the Stars been mostly in Our EYES as we clung to a Vision sold to U.S. of what WEE cood becum INDIVIDUALLY rather than COLLECTIVELY and dat shit Tore Niggaz apart Wee wanted to be Individual CELEBRITIES baby OR Amerikkka gave Black Women a WAY they cood Make It without A Nigga by their Side since he waant gone be round no how THE Gubmint became a Sistaz MAN and KICKED Her Nigga aka Baby Daddy OUT da Muthafuckin House in one shape form fashion or anutha AND assumed THAT role in her Life TEMPTED Her then PIMPED Her to the HIGHEST BIDDER accused the Nigga of being a QUITTER when in fack we whudden around to be ANY THANG Black Men are LEGENDS in the HOOD butt the Legends are LIES that are MADE UP becuz Nobody knows the TRUTH and those that DO ain't Talking or they DEAD Niggaz are ghosts dead men walking Dead Men LOCKED UP Dead Men dont EXIST I turn mah attention to the Horrors of Home and what we cood BECUM butt We AINT due to the Fack that Those who are not US cum between US as the Instigator and Participator Decimator of US cuz they HATE US LOVE US when we FITE each other idiotically vehemently and they take bets on the outcum yadigg all the while sipping wine eating breaking bread lata our heads butt dogmas often be products of half-educated parasitic sick muthafuckaz hoo think they are omnipotent butt are onliest insignificant and one talkin such as me hoo of da enlightened niggahood of da hood now fried gentrified laid to da side wile me raising da veiled way showing they pulling coattails emerging frum da puss eye eventually into what u see mee doing now turns out imma ancient unrecorded uncensused uncensored nigga back fo mo assisting mah niggaz in they 4ward evolution yet i is ignored n dont mean shit butt when a white man starts rappin spittin the negroids amongst us pull out a pencil pen recorder n start taking notes dotting i crossing t like a muthafucka asking questions to his massa n shit yet our days are not long upon this HOOD we cant afford the HOODTATION poverty politricks that we in the thick of the ick of not sitting side by side not walking stride for stride 2GETHER like we useta Do and Rule EMPIRES and Had POWER instead of bingewatching EmPIRE and POWER on Whiteys TV in his preowned section 8 shacks a cesspool of roach infested 2 bedrooms slummed in traphouses neatly lined up to be unlawfully raided by mercenaries see what had happened was Black Wommin took the BAIT sealed their FATE Niggaz got left at the GATE owned by BILL kontrolled by Special SEAL of the Federal Reserve involved in a Ritual we useta WADE in the WATER now we doggpaddlin to keep frum DROWNING we only be FROWNING at our own Disappointment even tho we got DEEP insites into our own SURVIVAL we dem CRABS not A-RABS in the BARREL memba that old Trick now U see it now U dont sumtimes U will sumtimes U wont watch it and chase it see where I place it MONTE HALL wit the DEAL of a lifetime CHOOSE DOOR NUMBERED ECOLOGICAL Disaster U BASTARD for the Nigga knowledge we cant git in Colledge thats our AVERAGE since we kno the Average Nigga that live onliest 24 heartbroken years then die every 27-seconds according to sum pensil pushing mediocre ogre balding in the middle of his eczema skinhead cubicle nazi nasa muthafucka who U aint never met yet involved theyself in a SITUATIONSHIP thats SAILED without U.S. never to return again

HOMELeSSness is where the HOPE is Long GONE Hope left me like a fart in a duststorm when I didnt give it hOPE or Evidence cuz I aint SEEN shit to GIVE it no hope in the first damn place then I FIRED mah self for I whudden a Self-Starter and HIRED mah Alter EGO to think bout The MAN I AM said to be according to Divine Rite of Kings who usually Die at 33 and 1/3rd on the 25th of erry monf be membered for eons doe as sumbody hoo done sum Important shit that nobody will every understand except in whispers and forgotten notebooks streams of paper and Intellectual masturbatory ooze in yo earhole I want u take that shit back u said in apology to an enemy cuz u thawt sumbody u kared about was looking n U wanted to Impress them wit yo random kindness u had read in a book they dont follow dont read where we frum there is still sumpen in what I said if U read between the accomplished LIES bitter truth and the LIEN on mah Spirit due back in the niggaz body I borrowed it frum for the trip into this theme park sumtime in back in the future of mah present tho im running late cuz eye got shit to do wit it B4 I give it back to him better than when I RECEIvED ET frum him For i came here not to be a FRIEND of the LAW but a FOE to Tear Down its STATUES and STATUTES SHOOT NOW Never Answer QUESTIONS Later for what U say will be used against YOU in a COUNTERFEIT COURT of lawlessness just perjurious bullshit masquerading as righteousness instead of the bloated despotism it is cuz wee all kno yo RIGHtS skrimf were born inside you soon as u became the GLEAM out ya Daddy I crystallizing formed according to the RECIPE that called for a REVOLUTIONARY type-a-NIgga be Birthed onto this plane who wouldnt be PLAIN but COMPLICATED and DIFFICULT to the Status Quo full of them Institutionalized Hatecism fo Catechism kinda folks tom bout ALL LIVES MATTER until its time to go to Skool git a Job buy a House or git Sentenced but least theres a SIGN for that See the DEMISE of Niggaz that count has been ERASED which aint no accounting for unless U tally bananas the shit up yo self like in this joint not that wee belong we just think we doo cuz we died defending a Banana Republic that used to stand for sumpen now has fallen for anythang aint worth falling for and this is the TALE OF 2 NIgGAZ OF 2 DIFFERENT BABY DADDYS 1 MAMA LIVING ON PARIS & LONDON STREETS IN ANYWHERE AMERIKKKA FORCED OUT OF THE GHETTO DUE 2 GENTRICATION IS REALLY NIGGA RELOCATION in DISGUISE happening rite under Yo EYES dont see what U REALIZE cuz its a tale tole furiously of huge signification bout nuthing excepting if they want it to be regards a nigga promiscuity then they find a white bitch to start rico acting yelling rape n racketeering wiping boogaz on the witness stand cuz if a nigga exists he exists in a form amount that kan be measured butt not like LIGHT wee too fast for dat butt like as guilty at first SIGHT Yet today as I Live and BREATHE the same air denied FLOYD & GARNER I write to fight another day for nigga nationalism when I thought the bell sounded to end the round 200 years ago or sumpen like dat **a Nigga has to be 6 different versions of his self on one hand and Half-A-Dozen more on the other hand plus an Invisible Muthafucka to git by talented 10th negroids** dont count since they aint shit despite the fack that We be da Bag Holders of the Insecurities of a Warring Race built on blood shame misery and whodunnit they aint telling we aint figgering it out either baby see weez liable for a guilt that aint ours in these realms Niggaz are NAIVE in dat way naive urban noble savages yet we invented unduplicatable ROYAL PURPLE peep the game bout dat so u kan truly know what our alchemical attitude is built upon when the rumors start that alternative narrative shit like the Jews aint the only ones suffered in World War 2 Niggaz was in the back of hitlers ovens just like we in da back of MR HYMIES ODE to a HOLOCAUST as a rule I aint got nuffin to say bout this it just needs to be said sumpen for the head ya digg butt these thangs soon cum to lite when u rite where u posed 2 B lissening like hoo woulda known niggaz was on da thrones of europe until we were thrown off by a lie that was round da world by the time niggaz were of substance hoo woulda known that by da Time JESUS showed up niggaz had already been crucified died and laid to da side of history they dont tell u dat Jesus first sermon was bout how the churches were originally made for fucking practicing tantra and downward doggystile and U couldnt git no parts of da pussy if u were a bitch nigga Now Bitch Niggaz git ALL da Puss Eye cuz Real Niggaz became an Extinction Level Event an extinction-level event also known as a mass extinction is a widespread and rapid decrease in the bioDIVERSITY on Earth and hoo mo diverse than da Black Man I ast U dont answer dat if U aint answering properly cuz I aint tryna hear dat shit not TO-DAY not Too-Ever not no never mah point is Authentic Niggaship is gone Missing Royal niggaz died out and dried out rather than THIRST after WATERED Down Consciousness passing for BLACK LIVES MATTER posturing which is just as useless as NO JUSTICE NO PEACE & KEEP HOPE ALIVE if we gotta tell em Black Lives Matter THEY dont whats understood dont need to be Explained for Gain or to Pain Prick those who cant be Pricked but are ONLY pricks who git their KICKS hitting below the belt or when a Sap is Down on his luck without a buck or twos n fews reported by the noose to be hangin n swangin in the breeze from trees wit a storee of peeps in every branch n leave im so disgusted wit religion i dont even fuck in the MISSIONARY POSITION no mo & if a bitch yell out Oh Mah God when she cum im Jealous cuz god aint da one hitting u wit this DICK upside the head n in yo mouf as u taste me & lift yo hips so i make partake further into da back of da pussy threading it like a needle til the juice fall out yo folds to behold that aint god thats me n im ignant bout mah fucking dat god aint nuffin to do wit so why even brang Her into it fo i will fuck her lata if she want it she kan git it too all them angels kan fack I heard heaven is feminist anyway ran by a bitch name LILITH on that METOO shit so niggaz like BILL COSBY & ME aint welcum beyond the HYMEN AMEN let us Pray cuz niggaz think PRAYER Changes Thangs dont know dat U caint Pray every Thang Away werd U caint Pray hardly nuthing started by crackaz away nowadays while we are being PREYED Upon as is our m.o. so it kan be Bizness as Usual we dont notice dat Peeple mostly Pray B4 they EAT or DIE Not good ODDS hell we never even ran the CIVIL RIGHTS MOVEMENT either kontrolled by alleged white liberals looking to enslave Negroes to their way of Thinking bout society upward mobility & access to THEIR shit including their White Women which the only reason a lotta white women joined the movement was to git fucked by Big Dick Civil Rights workers n invite Black Power into their bed for breakfast basically WHITE PUSSY brought down the Black Community cuz who among kan refuse a Purrty White Bitch wit The Bluest Eye Toni Morrison tole us bout not-a-one or not many fo sho except ME white pussy like overcast days never turned me on like that I dont even like sticking mah FINGA in white narrow shouldered pussy altho I will accept help frum white pussy cuz im always set to Lie to advance the Cause of Niggaz aint that what COINTELPRO did to advance the Pause of Niggaz surrounded us wit Talented 10th Negroids who fessed up all they knew bout Niggaz to the Gubmint bout eVERythang they could memba including when a Niggaz took a piss shit shave like nonredemptive jews whose conscience will never be for peace killed JESUS hoo was SOCRATES in a previous life traitorous sullied negroids killed MALCOLM with help from player hater MINISTER FARRAKHAN fanning them flames he apologized for cuz Niggaz in Religion and Political moovements written on yellowed paper backs of napkins old envelopes are just as unpardonable unnatural turncoats hoo aint never cumming back as Niggaz in RAP like GAY-Z JAY-Z DR GAY DR DRE which we Rap in but we dont own we just rap bout it but we dont OWN what we rappin bout just white kids listening n kontrolling means of production distribution no rap SKOOLS we just rapping FOOLS uneducated still bout our Intellectual Property wee back to the Lynching 1920s in how we think bout whats ours wee uneducated fools from uneducated schools so said see prophet Curtis when u consider the factors wee being kontrolled by political crisis actors students of hegelian dialectical defiant fists bullshit for deceiving muthafuckaz butt back to the moovement that we dont own in the streets shouting Black Lives Matter tho thats whats the matter we act like we scared to let Black Power cum out of moufs full force into the face of the established hierarchy we sced to take it back to black so wee lack power better yet take it to NIGGA POWER cuz Amerikkka is always sced of a KRAZY Nigga wit sum SENSE of who S/HE bee when Niggaz was actually REVOLUTIONARY not just their THINKING you dont memba dat shit when Niggaz useta raise their fists now we sced to raise our voice when black wommins let their hair git NAPPY on their Heads as well as their pussies if white bitches kan burn they bras on the lawn black wommin need to start burning they PANTIES in the streets to show muthafuckaz they actually factually kontrol the PUSS EYE belonging to the Black Man once again cuz now it dont BLaCk PuSSy belongs to RACIST MR CHARLEY now thats a DREAM deeper than KINGS instead what we have is a bunch o black lives acting like they matter full of COONscious gay politickal reverend chicken wang choir sangin wee shall overcum arm n land locked degreed so smart they dumb negroids wit church assumptions running away frum n towards a presumptive Revolution Niggaz thought we had is just a distant memory nowadays a wisp of a stinking fart left behind by them Negroes who thought or least acted like they were doing sumpen gitting us to spend Black Dollars with JEWS now A-RABS hoo took over most of the hood businesses that Jews left behind for the A-RABS stopped hijacking planes started hijacking black neighborhoods at retail n the Civil Rights act like White Feminists & Faggots everybody did fo real even the so-called Native Americans on the Reservations n Hispanics Faggots done went viral so far as to even have they own FLAG n Niggaz aint got one what kind o shit is that I ast U dat niggaz died so other muthafuckin ethnic groups could walk on top of our shit claim it thats why wee the only one gotta hold up signs tom bout WEE WEE Matter Cuz wee dont cuz when we HOLD UP HANDS cops still shoot first brag later bout they BAGGED SLAUGHTERED dem one u know its bad when PIGS doing the Slaughtering instead of BEING slaughtered at for bacon yet when word gits out that niggaz wannabe SEPARATED frum Whitey due to his BEASTLY nature that he cant kontrol or keep on a leash properly every time the MOON git FULL tilt he loose his mothafuckin mind a fack he been making clear wit dem WEREWOLF and VAMPIRE BEOUWULF mythological movies he either out for MONSTROSITIES or out for BLOOD disrespectively irregardless both Moon and Sun fuck wit him the Sun is the LITE the TRUTH shedded upon him and oooweee Whitey cant walk in the UV anonymously unanimously without gitting burned he aint learned he gotta squash the truth out by taking the blood of niggaz House NEGROES donate they shit willingly tho watch his movies kno that U cant SAVE-A-WRETCH like him yet WEB Too Many Initials DUBOIS peeple keep telling us this shit memba FRANKENSTEIN was a movie bout a KRAZY JEW written by a krazy ass delusional 16 year old white Bitch thats why the Diary is called ANNE FRANKENSTEIN shood be the whole name of anutha 12-year old white bitch hoo aint even exist but just let U know how far the JEWISH mind is willing to go to hipnotize feed a nigga lies and that shit got the whole wide world feeling sorry for sum shit that never happened to them but a bas relief belief got dem deceivers a nation called ISRAEL aka IS-IT-REAL no it aint if u sposed to git a nation based off Bible Myth then Niggaz deserve TWO or THREE of them Muthafuckaz nations anywhere in the known and unknown world including MARS cuz thats where we frum troof be tole why U think them big ass Olmec heads n lipps down in mexico niggaz escaped frum PRISON PLANET EARTH long ago we been going to and fro frum this Joint yaunderstandme leaving clues BEHIND for the remaining ones of Us to FIND KNO that we been heah B4 will be heah AFTER we BC AC Niggaz aka Yoda Yo Mama nem flew VIMANAS WHEELS IN MIDDLE OF OTHER WHEELS UFOS edged in new Cosmologie see JOB JOHN THE BAPTIST Rap This see the vision decision JESUS Conceived Received n Revealed wit his Daddy in the last book or werds to dat Effect that have taken Affect upon all Us Left Behind like it say the shit has not only been WRITTEN its been SAID cuz wee BAD in that WAY so doo what We say then put the RESIDUE Inside New Niggaz cumming upon earth birth marks let u kno too it aint all what you know its what u memba that is if wee kan butt keep the insane psychotic repressive Culture frum SNATCHING it OUT of U.S. like Big Mama nem wood snatch a KNOT in Yo ass when U misbehaved they knew da play if u lissened close not almost useta say JESUS was in AMERIKA teaching Niggaz the whole truth & nuthing butt the Truth so help his FATHER the Middle East is Middle America MISSOURI where the True NILE RIVER flow as The MISSISSIPPI ask the MORMONS they know just aint saying butt read their BOOK of THEMSELVES ask the BLACK JOSEPH SMITH not the White One tho same with JEHOVAHS WITNESSES them Niggaz leader was buried under a Pyramid on da otha side geometrically according to Euclid cuz he knew wouldnt tell yet they still knocking on Niggaz doors putting boots on the ground in hoods for that reason dem Sistaz still on da Stroll fo dat reason ALL these so-call Religions is really RELIEGIONS that have LIED about the Niggaz place in em so we dont know hoo wee bee in em kicked Niggaz out da God Head got Us GIVING Head crying tears busting slob to a PINK muthafucka of their choosing and losing saying he OURS nah he aint Ion know dat FOO U dont neither down to da Bone Yet they want you and me to chase ascension in they churches and buildings instead of descending into heaven between each-um-others legs thats why its Hell when U aint fucking the true Temple is the FORNIX deep in the Pussy but U dont go there so U never git properly Baptized filled wit the MOST of the HOLY GHOST after a while wommins gone be able to fuck themselves n git Pregnant No Nigga need apply dont call me angry i aint angry im mad im driven insane in the membrane by what i have seen these many years now my lips n dat lil thang dat hang down in da back of yo throat are like an old nigga wit Dementia hoo says what he want cuz he aint got no filter U wouldnt like me if I was actually angry hulkstering down on Amerikkkan Foreign policy FOREIGN meaning the hoods U ever noticed that NATIONAL GEOGRAPHIC been erry where but the HOOD n sertain niggaz bout to go extinct in fack, many HAVE already but it aint being reported cuz they dont go there just to die too badd FLINT WATER either or TUSKEGEE Experiments or The next HENRIETTA LACKS project for power they be sneaking into dem Underground Labs wit da help of JOHN HOPKINS n nem or the CDC WHO FDA RED CROSS VAMPIRES n yo local aint no FUNeral Home caught up in da PLOT to Disappear Black Amerikans then wonder why we ain't in the CENSUS cuz wee know it dont make no muthafuckin Sense to Us no how tryna COUNT Niggaz U caint FIGGA out they send MERCENARIES like THEIFS in the NITE butt they be dressed like Social Werkers wit Good Intentions butt Memba what Mama said the road to hell is paved wit Good Intentions and Badd Directions and its all Mapped out in that Enemy of Mines MIND so innerstand the REALITY we have been taught as real is butt a Figmentation of the Crackkka without Pigmentation Imagination that they actually have NO Proof that the UNIVERSE they have told sold U.S. as Real even EXISTS outside an EQUATION they Made Up in a LABORATORY STORY now Sponsored Supported n Promoted by a Monolithic commercial paradime of gubmint lackeys flackeys slaves coons samboes who bow when His Caucasoidness MASSA enters the room to Fire the Last Hired Niggaz U wood think that Muthafucka had done read scripture that talks about The LAST SHALL BE FIRST cuz I fell for that n HOMELESSNESS became mah Domain mayne on Main Street Yuba California was CRACKED off COCAINE ass out in the RAIN had me a 2 bedroom cardboard box tho courtesy of 2 Faggots name Jules & Jerrys Furniture store slept in jacked off boff upright n supine stole walking fast BEGGED relentlessly unashamedly desperately hungrily SOGGY SAMMICHES out da Dumpster is sum Beautiful-Tasting shit when its got mustard hold the Mayo cuz that looks like sumbody Cum 2 Me butt I ate ya digg I fought ya digg what U sposed 2 do when a Nigga wannabe taking yo spot u been sleeping n pissing in for 40 days n nights of fright wit pet rats gone git ya homeless pussy is still good Pussy too when u aint had none but yo righteous left hand for a companion share a used beer mixed wit PISS fuck in a compromised position catch the CLAP APPLAUD Yo Self that U Came at last Came at last Thank God Almighty U Came at last fast as u could u showed up at the CLINIC showed yo ass so the dreadful white bitch could STICK a needle in ya dick dat dirty unwashed muthafucka leave Yo ego in the waiting room when u pick a number to be called please butt see u next Month wit a new case of sumpen i want the strongest shit yall got back there so thats why I never ate raw wett pussy or drank the juice on an empty stomack got turned off dat 1nce I saw a bitch wit fleas maybe it was gnats same fam one time she even had a collar then i hitchhiked to a farm saw a nigga fuck a mule doggystile which I ane think niggaz did shit like that butt down at the bottom of society where the Foolish gnash teef chew the inside of their MOUFS to pass time u see dat type-a-thang growing immune to how u feel after seeing ya own life aint shit where it 1nce was u caint judge lest u be judged found wanting this shit take Yo SMILE U Grin n Bear it if U kan to The Man 1nce I fell outta the Air Force for insubordination wit insufficient funds aint no fun out in Cali wit No Beverly No Hills U gotta climb to prove Yo self outcheah to Yo Self always ret to eat n run snatch they food off the table they never see me cumming only see me going back in the wind wit the dust and farts I eat rice one at a muthafuckin time to make it last in mah memory fought a nigga to the damn near death over a lone bone B4 it was gone violence shone itself as normal rape aint a crime its survival not to me cuz I die before I let da soul of mah bootyhole be an entrance instead of an exit for the shit I have to put up wit n cum out of it in mah mouf if i aint had nuthing else to eat as manna see niggaz wit no Manners n lack of home training ready to run a Train wit Big Dick Willie as the Caboose using old chicken grease as a Salve or whatever they Have for the dirty deed high off weed wine n PCP water it dont matter its whatever mah sole reason for surviving was to live wake up and mah tongue wasnt mah own it was wooden like it belonged to a dummy there was no hand up mah ass butt I still felt like a puppet on a string tho sum days i whudden strung out hung out yeah Niggaz was always seemingly doing two thangs in the hood fucking and dying all the seasons were the same Open it all made sense as one nigga was dying anutha nigga was being born to balance the scales of Injustice a Nigga had waiting on him either way he go cuz Wee birthed blessed wit Civil Rights or civil RITES or the RITE to be CIVIL for Begging for Crumbs we still the BUMS tho so smile when U outcheah Protesting so they kan have Yo UGLY face on Camera wit yo missing back teef foo its a game that U dont see cuz U caught up on an Ideal pitched 2 U on the skrimf of upstanding 800 credit score white racists name of BF SKINNER HEGEL hoo shaped yo life of strife hoo made u look dirty crooks made U think when U Graduated Lawd Hab Mercy frum one of their Camps wit the other Tramps u was sumbody so U fell in love wit the appeal of the ideals implicated in Lady Liberty and the Bitch dont even SEE you to pay U no mind she let everybody else fuck her except Niggaz she wanna chain us up at her stankin feet then ask why we tired and yearning Bitch Ion even know what Yearning means in this scene written by minds there aint no reasoning wit cuz U cant reason wit Whitey thats kool except most Niggaz dont innerstand that you CANT so stop trying and u will stop crying real fears then tears will leave you and run backwards down yo face as yo courage cums forward and gird yo loins wit a new understanding of what had done happened was Niggaz be krazy off cough syrup drug dealed out by the worlds biggest drug dealer CVS WALGREENS a foo hoo name of DUANE READE on EVERY KKKorner & every Commercial cuz them treasonous Cambridge Analytics say our bloodstream is mo susceptible to whatever they create to wanna put in it to hook us we addicts to the addiction affliction butt mah fetanyl dealer is a white suburban mom hoo teach at the local colledge wit other Epidemicians ruled by the fire of desire that starts in the bones lodges in the sinew courses thru da viscera and roots in ya brain as a necessity of full blown Addiction drugs follow the same yellow brick road as fantasy when the 2 halves of ya Ruby Red mind click 2gether sealing the freshness of it all in place to taste must not waste even one drop so U stay sleep in Massas bed keeping him warm so no harm cums to him Negroes be protective of the Enslaverer the abused love the abuserer in love wit the habit cycle of misuse in order to pass it down in they genes butt it aint a curse we just USED to da shit love it miss it if U take it cry lik a baby without a pacifier living even now as a denier Yo peeple was ever Freedomkind there was never a Bind except the incessant one learnt as FundaMENTAL gospel commandments kept Holy Safe Secure as Gods RAP frum all alarms that Samboes sound when a Nigga go for freedoms sake knowing that White Folks train dogs to hunt bite n kill nigga figgaz canine cop dogs today got mo benefits than a nigga see

PETA mo respect let a dog die n watch Crakkka Cry like niggaz cry when a black man is killed the measured tears is the same amount let-a-Nigga watch Whitey take a vacation and read bout how he got away wit it cuz he hiding behind a BADGE instead of a SHEET that me an mah girl wood normally fuck on Butt this BITCH i tried to teach so we could avoid fucking all the time like she liked to do in lieu of nothing else we cood ever git 2getha on cuz the wizdom tween-a-Nigga-and-his-woman is soon departed under the cirCUMstances of Cumming and Going since most times thats where yall meet at and that shit dont change from pillar to pillow talk she feel good as long as the dick behave and stretch her shit out fuck her relentlessly to an inch of her strife relieve sum shit trapped in her pelvis flo cuz thats what the dick doo butt aint no convo for a nympho a well-read dick is useless to a woman that just wants to fuck and see how close she kan git to persuading U off yo mission of DOING SUMPEN productive other than pulling her hair cutting her air off while bombing one orgasm after anutha and saying yo name instead of Gods then it be over and she want you out in 5 below zero weather when U aint compliment her right after she fucked anutha Nigga the same way wit the ghetto kama sutra u taught her now u ass out clothes left money stolen she even kept Yo CUM inside her walls for the next Nigga to compete wit when he wave incense n black soap before her eyes n spit revolutionary poetics semen in her face thinking it matters for Niggaz are Naive when it cums to Voting wit their Dicks it dont butt thats for HIM to find out U know already that the Death of the Black Relationshp between a BITCH and Her NIGGA is not a RUMOR its REALITY that happened soon as Niggaz got the RIGHT to EXPRESS themselves see chuck wright n drank frum the same water fountain as White we lost our thirst for justice and Thangs Fell Apart even tho ROME WAS NOT BUILT IN A DAY The Hood Was Tore Up Over Nite according to the will of the Gubmint thats why the same problems exist n bitches giving pussy to their Uncle Sam doggystile while he pull on their Kitchen they dont cook in no mo they boil water in the muthafucka only to throw it at they baby daddy during a local state n federal argument in anger under house rules on a full stomack without directions wit closed eyes wit food particles on her tongue cuz she saw that shit in a Tyler Perry movie thats hoo bitches listen to then run tell the child support peeples U ran off & dat aint even what had happened but yo Bill $1 Billion Dollars in arrears u caint spell so u never git in front of again unless U became a statistic likely wit Corona lookin 4 U in the daytime wit a Flashlite since it work for the State Wee constantly fall for the OKEY DOKE not seeing you cant Fuck For Free there is a Fee having a Job gone Cost you yo Pee soulution git a vasectomy dig em out irresponsibly all up in them guts leave ya nut print on em hangin while you bangin da broad slowly drum her into submission wit her permission permeating she nauseating but you horny so stroke her so the pussy stay available for the block for the community thats hoo she be a place to drop seeds for the collective of no good Niggaz of wich you one for these purposes is not like the other X mark the wet spot Y you cum at the end if she does fair exchange aint no robbery thats how divine nigga attributes evolves thru mismatch mistakes and you git a nigga dats gone be sumbody not born Frum da Pre Cum and aint shit for an eternity of arrests ya digg 1 of these days U will cum to lean not unto Yo turned off Understanding short-circuited as it were by a long line of brainwarshed elites u gave way too much dap than they deserved so they cood turn Yo HATE inward against Yo self now U madd at Me cuz i aint quitting steady spitting flames upside the name of all that You been taught to luv down to yo no good mama nobody ever dared tole u strate up bout ya daddy either the 1st Idols that need to go you built up frum the floor up when ya mental was retarded white peeple say autistic niggaz say RETARDED cuz we know when a Nigga is truly fucked up butt the white ego is so FRAGILE they try to make it less so even a crackkka trailer park trash kid kan git a check while a Nigga crumb snatcha go RETARDED without a dime to his name seeing as how it aint in da Budget even the diseases are racist a Nigga is LAZY butt a lazy white bitch only got CHRONIC FATIGUE and a Organization a billion dollars to support her ailment wit assayed refined medications tested on little

Guinea Pig snotty-nosed african nigga children near where Kunte Kinte growed up to lose a foot to Capitalism in hollywood cuz slavery was invented in the HIStory books ONLY by JEWS lookin to sell Niggaz Post Traumatic Slave Syndrome while they paid themselves off in HOLOCAUST HOAX DOLLARS and a 6 million bedroom house wit a big backyard liveable gaza basement no I aint AntiSemitic thats Anti-Myself if the 1st Semites bee Niggaz of the 1st Kind hoo lived on earth when it was 1st Formed frum mist please notice dat Niggaz and 1ST go 2gether butt that fack is hid a lott in HIStory not OURS tho we kno not frum the pages of a book you Turn butt frum the book that Burns deep inside Niggaz KING JAMES BROWN VERSION also known as the HOLY BOOK OF NIGGAMASTE that says The NIGGA IN ME RESPECKS THE NIGGA In YOU This Just In dont 4git We were ROBBED of 12 MILLION ACRES and they wanna give us back 40 ACRES and we sposed 2 B Happy n Nappy like Niggaz caint Count like Niggaz caint Sign Nuthing butt an X cuz we dont kno Nuthing frum Nuthing leaves NOT-A-THANG see BILLY PRESTON who warned U.S. fo he left the Building and went back home to let em kno we still going thru it wit the PINK PEEPLES feelme and our relations continue to suffer from a kinda perversion we aint hip to cuz except for a small smattering of black men n wommins who have the integrity to create something tangible the Black Relationship is DEAD as a corpse laying askew in the bedrooms of Niggaz as 2 Zombies represented by the black man and woman Wee are two dead Niggaz fighting one another over a life that cant exist at all if it cant exist as something we build 2gether in this muthafucka Butt we dont know that because we have been blinded by the flashlight of the bullshit Whitey shined on the wall and showed us the rabbit tricks as something glorious so wee the natural born enemy of each other shall never be as one like we were in our fairytale associated wit Afrika most Niggaz aint even cum from Afrika ruling royally ruling side by side as man n woman on some Solomon & Sheba shit What the Pimps among U.S. understand that the average Lame Simp (male or female) does not understand is that society is no longer set up for niggaz to git along in beautiful relationships there bee only bitches hoes n bitch niggaz then there are pimps playas pussy persuaders like me or your local state or federal government ya dig who understand the game of life how to play it yaunderstandme it wasnt til much later in these twilight years of my life that the lites came on now I find myself in the same position that many of you Niggaz may be in today twixt n between listening to reason or damning oneself to a predictable miserable end thus u will find within these few words a form of spit fire that deals wit life liberty property n infinite fucking designed to brang to the forefront of yo mind the necessity for a revolution in yo stinking thinking thought forms as they relate to living in the Amerikkka of our births cuz so many of our Niggaz are headed for sertain damnation ruination at the hands of The Powers That Be who kontrol a Niggaz horizontal vertical up & down so that he or she doesnt even have an understanding of their very own Life of course many of these tenets dropped n slopped here had their genesis in the world of pimping frum which i cum for what is life except One is either Pimpiing or being Pimped Or One is either fucking or being fucked over one is either playing or Being played in other words as much as this book is about the GAME of LIFE its about PIMPING or being PIMPED as the case may be so that when U read these werds may your coat be pulled even as the wool is pulled from over yo blind eyes to the Illusional delusional you are living under in Amerikkka this is part of the wisdom that now resides within my skull passing on to you in the form of this drop that wont stop even after U close the flap cuz if u let it this shit will sink in and take root in ya mind ready to be booted n suited wit not only sense but uncommon sense since u been born that No nigga heretofore has laced u wit butt read this as a Nigga not like they taught u to read in skool in a linear fashion these are thoughts drips drops water on a rock to break down but not destroy the cock block in yo funny mental the White Boy put there he dont care butt let what I say play in ya synapses thru ya naps as a natural occurrence to a Nigga second nature u kan nurture into sum truly revolutionary mooves u will make based on this new evidence ya dig 1nce you git it in ya deep understanding you then know that the black race has been overrun wit da Bitch Hoe Bitch Nigga Lame or Simp sindrome nary a Real Nigga or Niggress black man or woman kan hardly be found on dry land in this muthafucka thats where you and i got to cum in and be the change other Niggaz dont see n will never see if you and me dont be that muthafuckin change but we aint doing it for them we doing it cuz the shit must be thy will bee done and cuz thats what wee were sent heah to do find each other in this morass this babylonian sodom n gomorrah konneck that means Real Niggaz gotta watch out for the Enemy created by the White Man which is the bitch or hoe so real niggresses gotta watch out for the vaunted bitch nigga wich is a Negro Black Man wit a PUSSY but he gotta Dick too but he really a pussy ass negroid and especially the Lame Simps among us must watch out that they are not taken advantage of by not being wise hip to the games that bitches hoes or bitch niggaz play so they git taken for all they got in dignity soul and whole existences if often fucked up behind dealing wit these type a negroes who are made in the laboratory wit birth control pills deprovera tilapia fish red dyes sprankled chemtrails over the unfortified ungentrified part of the city off the titty affecting a bitch fallopian tubes niggaz spermatocytes so these type a muthafuckaz caint help but be cum into existence in the lining of a hoe stomach among the living dying wind up being sumbody significant art of speech as they them or sum e vicious cycle continues cuz thats that shit up with Sergey Brin so U kan see what him and Bill Gates up merely one of many agenda and transgender of it what who knows what these muthafuckaz are now in the LGBQT most aint cute tho yet they gots a FLAG and niggaz aint and wee sposed 2 B a nation within a nation butt gay peeple aint never happy unless they steal affirmative action in the closet that mite be the key dont march or revolt be morose whine steal the Civil Rights momentum wit metoo white bitches make that ya dictum then dare sumbody to say sumpen wear pink ribbons outta Hitlers fabled ovens ignore the Niggaz that were there tho too in Hitlers backyard too paying a Helluvacost since dont nobody kno or will accept that Niggaz were living in Germany U heard of BLACK RUSSIANS welp Niggaz was there too so deep they made us a DRANK out of Vodka and hid the Shit in SIBERIA we in dem Mountains still wit mo cold freedom than heah in Amurica Morocco where yo Independence Flag is made in China in a sweatshop flophouse or Guatemala by an 8 year girl tryna git enuff so her Mama n Daddy kan steal-a-way cross the border and take Niggaz Jobs butt not our ass whuppings or splinters frum the brutal hands n nite sticks of the Police Puhleez If U aint katching on by now then u aint hip that REAL Shit requires a Real SHIFT so yo CONSCIOUSNESS will not be yo guide wrongly n not no longer be conned by the

CONstitution that THREE FIFTHS niggaz neve[r]
signed thats even a bigger con swindle bamboo[zle]
hoodwinked led astray shit that nobody ever or eve[r]
wanna talk about cuz it hurts their reality that aint
Real nowhere but in a european textbook psychotic
programming thats stuck in ya head as law butt
Jesus the Metaphor just the same real in substance
said she came to destroy the Law which them fake
jews by the way there is no Jew Land only Hymie
Town there aint No Afrika just a bunch of negroes
raised by a village idiot in the UN cuz it was carved
up by Whitey nem back round the same time they
was carving up Niggaz eating em as a delicacy ala
carte Im just the Messenger cleaning up the mess
they mess up Niggaz clean up whats left behind by
imposters who have tried to make it impossible for
niggaz to find out the truth & be able to authenticate
the falsehoods worn as white sheets that meet n
greet each other in private kabbalistic ballistic
lodges paid for by blood sweat tears of niggaz years
back ago when we owned the land jus soli jus scripta
jus sanguinis shit dat means its ours butt they say
shit like that in a dialect to deflect the creative
secretions frum their forked-tongue in the blueberry
of congress as tho they telling u true so we bleeve it
since we dont kno how to read tween da Lies n
Propagander or need the goose hoo laid the golden
egg on their faces they goose stepped U.S. and we
turned that shit into a Step Show cuz we Talented to
the 10th Power n feel PRIVILEGE butt thats those of

US hoo aint shit butt Tricks held up as ideal by WEB Too Many Initials DUBOIS as sumbodies butt wee aint shit butt an assterisk a white mans anamoly he likes to trot out when his circus cums to town needing a black clown to crown or negro hoe wit requisite PHD or MASTER behind his or her name or MONEY in their bank account so they kan be them DIAMOND n SILK black Cunts hoo caint die fast enuff cuz 1once U drank COON-AID You dont Die You multiply the lie for posterity since yo womb is filled wit White Mans cum so u dumb enuff to let em defecate in yo consciousness to soothe any guilt you mite have had now its flushed wit the cash you receive to sell out yo own that were never yo own under the circumstances bitches like dat love playing a funky feminist toon so their men git femi nazi approved first or they aint legit now he got the band round his ankle and gotta bite him foot off tryna escape Womanifesto metoo bullshit songs to trap a nigga cuz u got dem ones wit feigned black consciousness knowingly wanting to knock a nigga unconscious wit goddess pussy full of yoni eggs so special if man bleeves that pap smear rap however You scratch one of dem hoes deep enuff u reveal how they just wanna brang a nigga down to a shell of his former i self god dog him then report back to da Sistahood that there wit the grace of goddess go anutha one moove onto da next one cuz they line up cuz bitches smell like hoodoovoodoo incense egyptian musk shea butter virgin coconut oil the holy smell of consciousness pimpstressing that Simps Lames Game caint resist n that tempt the best of the rest even the very elect of the Niggaz We suffer due to our mistaken belief that Amerikkka kares for our BLACK bodies and NIGGA asses in a manner befitting citizenry of the soil butt this is not True and so it is not to be nor will it ever be our state in as long as we are in the State or Condition we have found ourselves in its a day that will live in niggamy infamy you rise to face anutha day that was granted to u on parole in this Year of the White Man Calendar for we are living in the way he expects Us you me we to be grateful for despite the poverty he got you existing in wit no car u know every bar cuz drink is yo solace to combat THE MAN who got all The Weapons Bombs Bullets make U realize You a hoe for the united states of pimping u wide open outcheah wit no benefits just an experiment hoo gone wind up in sum lab or sum old rich white bitch bloodstream to keep her alive awhile while U wonder what had happened to justice hope n fairness is mediocre memba that u fail wit erry thang fair trial = guilty fair fucking = a bitch dont invite u back into the Puss Eye again for anutha round of that sad ashy dick loving u came with the 1st Time round so it aint no rebound in this game of fucking n ducking wit no timeouts no clout scores romance without finance stands no chance u take love is a wake scheduled for deliverance to yo heart that u follow butt it dont follow u back it aint social like that so u hurt n seek the scriptures that say Do Unto Others Before Its Done Unto You is how they livin in Amerikkka mayne you aint kno cuz u slo distracted redacted subtracted contracted wrackted wit pain its a shame gone be the song at yo dirge at the urge u succumbed to will be written upon yo face while u lay in place in yo casket sharp as a muthafucka to other muthafuckaz hoo just wanna see anutha muthafucka like them they suppose since they think they know u and will say they knew u when all over again to anybody hoo ast em bout you its writ large bout u boo as a bitch wood say wich u hate butt bitches love being at odds wit a god a niggod thats odd 2 those hoo aint on dat frequency freakwency that u frequently frequent how You a boo if You aint a ghost scary to foes and fakes and faux and folks hoo aint real they sced to be tho so po beeyond poor so no door is open thru wich one may enter and return after respite rest recuperation a nation of niggaz bee tired mayne cleaning up after crackkaz hoo leave shit erry where and makes laws against litter and u n me bitter yet they titter tatter on niggaz big brotha stile 5th chapter of da Book done tole u how it was gone go in the future that has arrived when it was written for the experiences U now experiencing whole cloth at not wholesale U paying retail for an experience cuz its going thru a middle man a little man who profiting off yo pain since he in the middle of it selling you the yellow brick road no rainbow at the end just a pot of flowers **that mark a grave yours even tho its unmarked its got yo**

name on it had yo fame on it u popular after death got yo flower while U were alive to see it outta one eye blind in the other contradictions in diction up the yin yang out da ass mite be assinine to you benign bingo! to anutha muthafucka tho yo jackpot is a crackpots sanity different strokes for different fokes is how the werld werks when the world werks if it werks ya digg my nigg fraudulent virulent as ever as the naive who deceive themselves wit images illusory processes icons celebrities wee trust to tell us the troof the hole truth so help us cause god aint anyway never trust a god hoo aint got no wife to fuck missionary position what else wood a god fuck in anythang else wood be uncivilized but watch so that U realize that to gain peace requires war violence cuz summa da most violent warrior niggaz u ever wanna see were Priests who u think taught the world how to fight maim kill muthafuckaz wit arts of war while the sun was out zoo stile niggaz hoo aint turn the other cheek thats hoo cuz now they got U.S. turning the other cheek while they split boff cheeks wit no grease and a long handle spoon or plunger after they done used it on chadwick boseman black panther ass for AIDS research butt first a commercial to git U 2 support HAITI wich they hate altho the money and the hours are good when u traffick in children under the guise of the United Nation Shituation Red Cross takes the blood assigns it a number in a database based on whether its a lil nigga child or not monkeys n pitbull dogs git mo respeck than niggaz how do we know cuz a white man wood rather descend from an APE than the NUTS of a nigga hoo was a 1nce future king of bling now a botched civilization long ways away frum Noble Drew Ali wee aint noble savages weez noble averages below whom the bell curves 1nce it tolls aint no nigga safe or kno where to be hoo to ast fo what time to go to bed what set u frum homie democrat or republican democrackkka or repthuglican wit ties to disorganized slime you under arrested development u have the rite to be silent remains after all else has been taken frum u the little what is left is yours thank u 4 reading I kno u cood have been reading sumpen else and hope u read me again and if u dont fuck you very much this was never 4 u then muthafucka pass this shit on to sumbody hoo deserves it other than u foo yung Niggaz hoo speek the language of the embittered battered but not forgotten but forgotten by those in the axis powers i start u finish read tween the cowardly lion is niggaz u kno that rite thats hoo that was in the Wizard of Oz Niggaz caint roar no mo cuz we too scared to be king of the jungle that we live in so they gentrifying the muthafucka since we aint using it like Afrika where Tarzan was a a real estate agent hoo saw the potential and decided to kick Niggaz out and carve it up outswum niggaz hoo had been swimming in the Nile for hundreds of years yet never went to the Olympics to win a gold medal then they die n git backstroked to the beginning constantly rolling the stone back to the top of a mountain butt not like Sissys Fussing in heaven where aint no white folks cuz white folks dont belong in the same heaven as niggaz they belong in hell where niggaz kontrol the thermostat and 1nce again are most of the population butt these are most of the niggaz Crackkkaz incarcerated so they gotta spend an eternity wit dem Niggaz now and be in bed by 5pm central 4pm mountain or git wrote up by niggaz wit bad hand writing and strange fruit for lying bout how how niggaz died after they arrested em lest we forgit the prison industrial komplex is sponsored funded supported by neocorporatists you vote into Orifice and they be all in ya orifice for extended periods of time wit no relief cuz ya put em back erry time their time is up so they kan continue making money off the skin you in huemans mostly wit other races spewed thru out for diversity niggaz got the most jobs in the penitentiaries cuz they hiring us at record rates across states to make furniture n housecalls about the national debt set by Reagan Republicans acting the whole time like he knew what he was doing when it was Nancy pulling his strings and keeping his forgitful head up above water based on his horoscope aquarius hi my name is Ronald and i like a nigga hoo is obedient subservient n willing to do the samboish shit i want him to do and if thats u mah nigga lets git 2gether for a good time so we kan float float on rowing down the stream merrily in a life built on mah died fried laid to the supply side dreams of the future that dont include Niggaz like you in space or no place else hollywood helped me to create for wit ya nose open allowing me to see strate up into yo cavity this just in voting is in violation of Niggaz tendency to bleeve in shit they dont understand so they suffer the superstitions slings outrageous misfortunes instead of taking up arms against a heap o troubles thinking it nobler to die in their sleep rather than oppose em ending heartache natural shocks to the dome n flesh wit no heirs singed hairs consumed devoutly by a wish upon a star n dreams deferred like dried up raisins in the sun the coons among us dont see the oppressor as rong on the throng tho hoe niggaz be despised butt thats the insolence of Political Office once in they spurn niggaz advancements as rape harrassment fuck the kiss we just fucked unworthy now destined to grunt sweat a weary life in our sleep slim perchance wit that my nigga we are turned now one against the many others we know not of unaware wit no conscience that we are native hues of anutha yet in a moment of joy we be onto sumpen yet merely woes so we think but its just a pale capitalist fascist communist socialist company propaganda techno enterprise brought to us wit great pitch n slick regard and before you know it wee niggaz done lost a lot n our names then named the Sinners in a jesuit trial in which we shooda been the Winners lawd ham mercy these are facks see its a lie that turnabout is fair play it aint unless u the judge jury executioner otherwize its just a play game theory betting the odds YOU

LOSE the White House has the advantage fault is yours once the ball leaves the racket lands outside the lines not designed by you cuz most Niggaz dont kno that game dont play that game errything we doo in that realm is hail mary hoping for grace throwing ourselves on the mercy of the court ran by pedophiles fags n metoo perpetrators calling the shots as tho they are without a mark but hypocrisy hides behind black robes white sheets shiny badges n a blue wall of silence while U think it matters it dont it wont it cant and it never will its not in the Will and neither are niggaz positively posterity dont include you in the constitution preamble ramble even tho niggaz wrote the first one how U know cuz it was written on rolling papers while we smoked the Peace Pipe got left wit a piece of pipe now Amerikkka plays the lottery hoping to hit that Pick 4 straight or box and wipe out the national debt for pennies on the dollar except when mah ship cum in they got they hand out like I aint already give them 10 kids they use for cheap child labor still want me to support em but thats why I had em so they could uplift the ism of capitalism u claim u started Amerikkka what I make is for the need not the Greedy taxationing me without representationing or reparationing me still niggaz are the economy so gotta hussle and rob except we aint git the memo so we rob da rong muthafuckaz we the last hired n first robbed of freedom however we sposed to give the president a standing ovation when he walk in the room stand for a judge bout to send us to doom yo honor my papa was a rolling stone and that aint rite what U bout to do to me sending me to be entombed for 8by10 years all because im addicted to the shit yall sold me thus living the best way I kno how under the circumstances forced upon me by policies i read butt didnt understand so i signed em under pressure and penitentiary of perjury with mah blood since I aint have no brand name #2 pencil so I like to say mea culpa mea sorry mea fucked up mea dont kno what came over me after they hit me over the head when all I did was raise my hands in the air to ast a question niggaz aint afraid to git raped in prison cuz we git raped in Court first so our asses is ready for the sling the thing as it is for cell used some wear n tear by previous owner title held by the State Snakes make best offer of parole denied just because the department of Corrections has never been correct its entire existence which begs the question how kan u brang a clean thang outta an unclean thang darkness doesnt cum frum the light the light cums frum the darkness but the enemy hoo cums fum evil comprende not for light is not in them nor truth to tell u the truth ruth the makers of the Law are not the Doers or Followers of the Law these laws are made to order that which cant be Ordered or Ordained by Man and thus they tear down the fabric of society merely existing as a cliche n lip service the mouthpieces hoo turn out to be a violation of all the amendments promised to be upheld for niggaz on trial n the highest level of unfortunate triage the game has changed and the elevation of your consciousness is more important than the development of your body if u wannabe sumbody on dat old skool on ancient skool that will cause seismic shifts against wich there is no defense thats true sound rite reasoning u never heard before u felt before in yo veins mayne that collapse for the beat the heart makes so the blood like da bloods we are will brang down Babylon not with traditional weapons butt where upon sound will abound as long as we play at a to be determined decibel level that devils cant withstand to a man the justice scales fail n we have to employ the scales of music after we tweak em solfeggiocally trust they gone take this magic shit jokingly then the Laughter will fall like the walls that surround them have always fallen into empires of rubble anutha bubble of toil trubble based on sorcery n trickery witchery of the bewitched when long been U.S. cuz we were stuck on stoopid weapons we had no access to butt had success too already except we had no leaders or teachers of the darker arts who cared or cared speek what is now bout to happen into manifestation for the cessation of Evil as we have known it all our lives see wee bee those Last Nigga Figgaz that this country has not known what exactly to doo with Us when they cant Kill all of Us off on earth when wee have cum by more than a 10th of our Talents Abilities Gifts Skills TAGS in an Honorable manner butt wee are dealing wit a dishonorable gubmint that as long as we continue to expect them to give us sum respect we are in for a high form of dysfunction and a continuation of regress not progress as millions of US fall by the wayside as a result therefore we kan no longer tolerate this kind of Amerikkka wich has played out in the 21st century as the crackkka powers that wannabe want it to be that is a future that does not include niggaz like you and me as viable humanity no we are seen as a perverse appendage to be removed from the body politick wit the usual tricks of coercive corrosive corruptive Idolatry hegemony thus they keep the monies outta our hands in banks they store behind an invisible red line niggaz dont git to cross to be a boss or have self autonomy or do for self so we are lazy according to the welfare we receive butt its okay when the Enemy of our enemy gits paid for the same thang the double standard persists to resist such categorization condemnation as Whites are Lazy butt Niggaz are not if u bleeve the theories n stories that we built plantations frum sun up to sun down frum cant see in the mourning to caint see at night for no pay except cotton tee shirts that wee still pay full price for or if there is pay its in peanuts that wee invented to eat not cash out wit butt Whitey disputes that in a jiffy in the same old corporation cum plantation politricks they outlawed enslavement only to Niggaz being free into a criminal industrial complex enterprise called the 13th Amendment to keep U.S. at 13 percent or less of peeple since they tried to make sense of niggaz since the first census aint make no sense just nonsense all the fucking Niggaz have done and the Needle still stuck on 13 percent aint mooved on our population concentration because wee dont COUNT and the caint count neither Uncle Sam or Big Brotha always wanna know where Niggaz be at 3am on a random Saturday Nite special to fill an Agenda tho TUPAC was Rite 50 Niggaz is all U need and thangz wood Evolve at the Speed of FIGHT i know he was Rite n Exact cuz I saw him cuz I got as much Rite to keep seeing Tupac as Crackkkaz got to see ELVIS hoo Stole the cumplete essence of Jackie Wilson life like the Hound Dog he is then mooved into a Mansion based on precisely the same shit he hated Niggaz for collecting royalties never treated Jackie wit da same royalty or loyalty even our Intellectual Property is a ward of The Hate inherent in the State thats why they like to stamp n kontrol the Paperwork so when we say sumpen it dont Work snakes Speek wit Forked Tongues n crawl Real low on bellies cuz thats where they comfortable at that Niggaz aint seemed to git this shit thru to innerstand this in our heads enuff to git ahead of da game recup losses katch up frum a centuries head start gained chiefly thru cheating niggaz outta their Inheritance hoo have no Awareness of the Rareness of what wee doo n brang to the table that wee are not allowed to Sit down at altho those of Us hoo know dont want or wood never SUP wit da Enemy cuz wee kno wassup wit da enemy as well as the Enemy of Our enemies i personally git the fack that its hard for quite a many to stop showing undying love for our Abusers hoo use Us never choose Us same time wish they cood lose Us butt they cant loose niggaz to go for themselves becuz then there wood be nobody else to do their bidding no kidding those within our ranks hoo still chase the cheese Amerikkka puts in the trap for the mice and u and they kno who they are the White House is the Biggest Trap House that ever was run by the largest cartel that ever was killing the mostest Peeple there ever Will be at 1 time then blame it on Imaginary A-Rabs or Anonymous Russians China Men computers that the United States GIVES them the access to then wonder how they stole the Political Selection of the POTUS hoo already had notice that the shit was gone happen that way during the trade agreement deal that was reneged on that Marco Polo tole em bout 800 years ago thats how long China been planning Corona Virus strategy they themselves are Immune to since they first donated rats roaches msg n soy sauce to Amerikkka wit the help of The BRITISH Crown stiff upper lip service policies created under the Influence of Opium they smoked wit China and now grown in Athens Middle East of Afghanistan wit the help of anutha so-called Family Sheikh cheaters Mail Order Bride professionals and Peak Oil signs being ignored in favor of greed memba what Baba DICK GREGORY said aint no Oil in them muthafuckaz the rest is a Conspiracy of the highest order deepest depths like

Water costing Flint even tho its Dirty Hairy wit mildew wich will Do when its only Niggaz clogging up the landscape but cant escape the Rape Pillage where it used to take a Village to raise a Nigga now it takes the Penitentiary based on Niggaz paying Penitence for a sentence they aint even write let that explode in yo consciousness becuz the gubmint been droppin bombs on the black community for years including CRACK that decimated eliminated untold unlimited amounts of Nigga Figgaz hoo aint never done nuthing to them except be present and un-accounted for it was never a DRUG war it was a RACE war Seditious Act Amerikkka starts shit wit Black Folk using the principles of Dead Philosophers or as they call em GODS deified in rocks crosses n dollar bills wit an Eye open to keeping shit stirred up like stir-fried rice long as we follow SCHOPENHAUERS blind will leading the blind they happy n nappy its our problem wit da reaction they want The JEWS killed JESUS and NIGGAZ killed MALCOLM now what muthafuckaz those hoo rule aint looking for Balance they aint looking for shit but 4 U to line yo ass up frum in the Beginning like White God tole U or in White God U Trust but White God dont trust YOU foo Those hoo THINK are DANGEROUS those hoo Think are I AM those hoo Think cause problems wit EXISTENCE have a PERSISTENCE RESIsTaNCe to the ACCEPTED Way instead of the Natural NIGGA way of doing thangs this is why JUSTICE is urged against NIggaz we too

Persistent on being a Natural kinda peeple that signifies a Sustaining Capacity and Crackkkaz and the Traitorous Coons hoo help em dont want Niggaz to be SUSTAINED in no shape form fashion or be Kool they want us to Embrace Self-Deception in the Department of Corrections under lock n key while we ask how much more Falsity is still necessary to screw in a lite bulb if U answered ONE you rong cuz Niggaz aint never been MONO bout a god-dam thang DUALITY REALITY has always been the WAY of the Nigga Figga not DECEPTION wich is the Way of Whitey or per Langston the Ways of White Folks this is a discouragingencouraging werk if ever there was butt Niggaz are cumming out of A Great HiberNATION thawed if U will by thawts heretofore forbidden for us even to think bout regards our Elevation knowing as we know as Niggaz that The Internal Truths is just as great as the External Facks in short every Nigga know he knows what he knows and what he DOnT know he dont worry bout OUTSIDE his self and realizes or said anutha way katches enlightenment sees that shit is Rong in the long run Memba a seed of lie to truth adds to the mixture of the HIStory ya digg like a weak boxer in any fight a lie caint go the distance tho it may rise n shine like gold off top on bottom it aint shit this must not be forgotten is often said butt unfortunately too many Niggaz Un-heed this game I just explained for ya brain understood in when viewed in lite of all the shit unsound doctrines occupying the dome creating ghetto up against the worst of white trailer park trash ANYDAY blee dat shit or not its on U butt its the Nigga dat need reforming tho huh meanwhile Black folks aint never held nobody in Slavery but the real beasts of the Jungle claim they done had Niggaz as slaves and everybody else including locking U.S. up for breakfast lunch dinner n snacks The negroids among know this truth howsumever soon as MR HEIMY cum offer such kind a high position money n a lil power they forgit all bout Their peeple they accept the gratuity and reject themselves and their kind since they have fallen and caint git up in Amerikkka WEE outcheah doe searching for GOD thats already inside Self waiting to be discovered not like Columbus hoo aint discovered cuz thats what U call it when its done that way ast yo self this if U STEAL sumpen on Columbus Day is it actually STEALING or is it DISCOVERING let that shit agitate yo mind enuff and U will see this is how The Enemy arrives at a fucked up opinion bout life liberty property fucking n sertainly NIGGAZ the shit will stay perpetual fixed long as certain kinds of U.S. Black Fokes accept THEIR WAY as true sources of divine inspiration THEY say they have gained via sweat n perspiration instead of the lynching n bloodshed it was actually attained by ya peeping game understand that summa what Im saying aint obvious for OBVIOUS reasons if u aint figgered out why dont worry it aint 4 U or U prolly the Enemy done got hold of mah shit meaning its gone take more than a cursory view cuz I aint tryna flatter yo mind wit its precconceived notions of Niggadom or what a Nigga is such as I AM but being a Nigga has its advantages and effects not always seen to the Naked Eye or in this ERA so everythang aint for errybody and to be rendered accessible unto many kinds of mens minds no matter how much they look at this shit I AM GRATEFUL for the SOURCE CODE not available aint no favors here fuck the Multitude n the Attitudes and bitches in cramped apartments wit big asses hoo dont know what to do wit em cuz they scared of my Pimping thus they just katching sperm frum a veritable cornucopia of copulative Negroes dropping seeds babies hate an dDUMBOSITY in em hoo line up at their revolving door wit hard Dicks in hand koolaid msg cells ready to go in a HOE so she kan produce a BItCH ASS NIGGA to infect a new Bitch born simultaneously down da road among a crowd of white authorities this cycle MUST END so A Nigga kan cum to know how to be The MASTER of Himself never forgit most Niggaz been to hell n back and enjoyed it so we know the way have an opinion and the hood is worse peep game and U will never be da same as I drop this slop let yo conscious be yo guide for this ride thru my werds syllables notions potions so if it dont make sense to ya naked eye yo minds eye will katch it peep it and ya subconscious will break it down while U deep sleep upon waking into awareness dareness let it be uppermost inside yo thinking that those hoo rule U do by creating a reality based on some sorta hashed 2getha metaphysics morality religion pscience lies to subdue yo perspective for their own purposes among wich is to avoid paying niggaz for all the shit we invented and got the Patents to show for it 1nce they stop hiding them like Einstein was doing when he werked at the Patent Office stealing shit like the Autistic Dummy he was he knew dam well E=MC2 was in India under the aegis of Niggaz long before he claimed it as his own 1905 that was one Superfluous kike Ion like never have cuz the half aint been tole on him the outrageous thinking he posited on nature whudden even his thinking butt done got written up as so by his fellow jew boys hoo kan doo dat shit since they kontrol the magic media sorcery so he immunized against the real and U think EINSTEIN is a placeholder for Genius when its aints just anutha example how they make what aint exist against the Facks jack their history is full of such misleading theatrical icons Names Dates Places Events a lie agreed upon according to napolean hoo was just a lie himself a figment of sumbody imagination creation illustration made up in academic labs butt dead as a corpse in a slab fo real he never skipped to Waterloo in the first place so they love 4 Niggaz to absorb white fantastical wet dreams stay poor without never cumming to full knowledge of self realization which to Their mind is the lowest hierarchy of what a Nigga need to be full of some thing like a phenomenal being resides inside instead of seeing the Tricks for what it is Taught we were slaves so long next we be taught Niggaz came frum caves butt er body and they Mama know by now Black Folks never had no Neanderthal blue genes blue BLOOD cuz our veins always been too dark for that and our craniums too small to fit history like that or the bottom of Ships that LIARS n the MISLED in da Head wanna putt us on as Cumming To Amerikkka on Niggaz dont need HEAVEN we got that good Insurance in our Melanin yeah Niggaz got all the MELANIN butt White Folks got all The MONEY now what regroup Muthafuckaz regroup for a coup to recoup they gave Us The BIBLE butt the a BIBLE ain't Viable Liable or Reliable they gave us the KORAN yeah butt the Koran is Also-Ran Ran Down and unspecific non-terrific in hoo it loves to see pray 5 times a day they gave us JEHOVAH yeah butt Jehovah be rapping on Yo Door wit no Solutions just questions bout the Mulatto named Charles Taze Russell hoo started it then they putt their Bitches back out on the Stroll butt what if I tole U a fine Jehovah Bitch knocked on mah door and I fucked her on several pages of her Watchtower while she watched the Dick go in and out then I putt her out cuz She aint kno who Black Jesus was and why he dont appear in Quaran or why he BLUE in India (cuz he got Blue Balls) them Indians be holding dem Nuts too long in dem Yoga positions and it's hard to fuck a Bitch in dat downward dog ask Siddhartha he aint git no pussy he sat by a tree got ENLIGHTENMENT butt no Puss Eye they gave Us The Book of MORMONS butt the Moormons wont admit their Rapture is when Niggaz take over and git back on top n stop crying sitting on da curb when da World takes our apple punked us puked on us they putt Their mind in Our Minds so we caint think 4 ourselves only think LIKE them bout ERRY THANG and our Years are the Years of Our Lord the White Man thats how wee know what day time it is IT was invented to keep track of Negroes every day belong to Whitey excepting they give us 28 days in February cuz its too cold as a Muthafucka to doo shit outside except freeze Knowing god-dam well a Nigga need a full 30 days to cum up wit dat Rent money to afford staying in his SECTION 8 House The Lord giveth butt the White Man Taketh Away and then go WHUP Gods ass for fucking wit his Money Niggaz be praying to god and dont kno dat Whitey OWNS HEAVEN Cloud nine is really sum Uber ran by the Nazis butt when Niggaz was doing dat shit wit private rides it was Illegal now its a BILLION Dollar Bizness dat aint none of Niggaz bizness this shit aint exceedingly komplex its simple supreme mathematicks wit a causation rooted in racist reams of bullshit that must be reconceived to git a grasp grip n be hip to da pscience wee been HUSTLERS dealing not Rustlers stealing dont make no mind doe cuz Amerikkka dont Speek our survival Language outta their dualistic mouths all of our Healers Prophets been killed we LEADERLESS once MORE saving grace bee the Hive Mind tho there be difficulties wit dat due to a Virus in da Hood Nest goodness so we Thrive bestest wee kan down to erry man woman child for the conditions are not of our Volition violence virulence is silence the way they pay to play and Niggaz dont have a say less wee bee on sum Mama May I Simon Says he dont Like U so U eliminated off American WHITE Idol Worship where pink bitches hoo sang like Black Wommins git cheered on git signed to a contract instead of them just hitting a Sista hoo already hanging like a Sista butt thats what happens when U dealing wit da White Fragile Ego dat wont let go of da extreme Marginalization Game they live to play where Niggaz dont git GO past GO only a Git Outta Jail Free Card that caint be used cuz it Expired soon as a Nigga took a Board Walk butt are all white Folks Racist NO just MOST of em are all Niggaz good U already kno da Answer to dat Wee are just as Korrupted now our own worstest enemy bee Wee Selves still n until wee git Crackkkaz out da way we gone pay wit our Black Lives Mattering not treated like slick Snot on a doorknob dont mean I like the fack that I got more Black Enemies than White Friends what U expect frum a Man hoo is a piece of MANufactured Equipment nowdays at least cuz it whudden always like dat then when the Gubmint replaced God as the Creator of Peeple all that shit changed in the blinking of an eye on a dollar designed by scholars hoo hollered sum Deistic syllabic werds U never heard and thats all she wrote in as Law hold the emotions hold the let-us pray just HOLE up wit the one U wit if U caint be wit the One U SAID you loved while yall was on the Battlefield they wannabe yo friend long as U paying U kno the type Im tom bout do you KNO whatimtombout first of all Niggaz immune to most diseases especially CORONA which aint nuthing butt a Common Cold the W.H.O. said was UN-Common cuz Niggaz whudden Dying frum it so how Niggaz start Dying Frum Mucus dat only Asians was Onliest Ones gitting DEAD Frum at first so Corona leapted out Asian chests into a Nigga Bloodstream all da sudden now we Caint Breeve polluted air no mo Meanwhile aint no mo slanteyed Muthafuckaz being killed prolly for da reason they own TIKTOK round da Clock so they got sumpen on TRUMP since he be on dat Muthafucka under a false name talking to JEFFREY EPSTEIN after hours when he think aint nobody looking after him and his whole pedophile administration including da POPE Kanye West Madonna Eddie Murphy n Arsenio Hall Oprah n Gail Bill n Camille Russell n Kimora Will n Jada being Black AF while doing The MOST un-godly shit possible to sexually- trafficked children sponsored by the RED CROSS and every non-profit Organization known to man cuz thats what Non-Profits devoted to chillrens do they FUCK kids n sell em to the highest bidders in auctions set up by EPSTEIN then dem kids have da BLUES rest o they Life niggaz live wit da Blues as a friend confidant so when we sang em wee ain't depressed mad or NUTHING wee rejoicing in a friendship wit a friend hoo always been there and gone always bee wit Us helping You thru hard times good n badd sadd Butt not cuz U GOT da Blues butt cuz da BLUES is all of life wrapped up in an enigma messaged in a bottled of drank so when U see a a nigga dranking He aint got problems She cummunicating wif da Spirit of da Blues hoo resides in bottles like all the greatest Genies doo and U gotta call Him out so She kan cum DANCE n sertainly talk wif U bout what needa bee talked bout sure as U Bone or Nigga shoot up his Veins wif pain free absolution forgiving himself in the Land of Nod cuz aint that what JOB did n lived in da Land of Nod in ashes stankin in protest to a Fake God in da Land of Nod til god better known as HIS SELF answered wif an Answer bout how to put sum Money in his pocket summo til He knew how da werld was made so Niggaz wood know when The Enemy said Different he wood kno that DAT was sum shitty pscience NOT the Truth butt UN-TRUTHS in the werst way un-like the bestest way or The WAY of da NIGGA for LIES are the currency of the Un-Learned and take that how U Live cuz thats how U prolly gitting it too yo consciousness been gone so long its at large n wanted in at least one state U so un-enlightened U have no bulbs to go off if git an Idea or Ideology U immediately turn into an Idol to worship on Yo Wall or in yo pocket along wit yo Rabbits Foot Gris Gris Bag wich I stopped dating this Afrikan Bitch hoo had to putt Salt everywhere outside da Door BITCH me need that Salt for Seasoning this Season n U throwing it away on Perceptions that ain't even happened yet talkin bout betterment when U know better U doo betta U betta those that a lotta times cum outside they self but u ever notice that the Kraziest peeple tell the MOST truth U can git in one session wit em they line up truth like U aint neva heard it befo no lie this is sumpen Niggaz Understand inherently cuz we know dat 1 Nigga FATE is tied to dat NEXT nigga fate that is boff substance and evidence of Thangs seen and unseen so dat when a Nigga Consciousness die it cum back within anutha Muthafucka dat look just like him in SKIN color or Attitude cuz RACE ain't always bout PIGMENTATION butt bout ATTTITUDE and Stance how sumbody grounded n founded so U white n identify BLACK identify Nigga U black identifying white identifying CRACKKKA just dont try to play boff sides against da Middle doe be hoo U is n dont waver Frum it dont depart frum it KNO hoo yo Shituation rests wit yo pledge of allegiance I'm just droppin discourse baby ya digg that U kan take as nice advice and take it twice if U want 2 make sho da shit sink in to da Bottom of ya mind to git out frum under being SCAPEGRACES all the time wich kan only be avoided when Niggaz cum to da KNOWLEDGE of KnOWING that Illusion of inclusion has claimed our whole souls in many Dis-respects so wee fail to see the merits of marriage to da proper ideals often the ENEMY is Yo INNER ME rather than WHITEY butt if his Irrationality selfishness possessiveness greediness petty intrigues are inside Yo head its really da same Thang tho aint it Basikally its time 4 AMERIKKKA to DIE for Niggaz since wee done died for Amerikkka so god-dam much and for what the Rite to go to Skool wit the Barbarians that many of them are wee go fight in American Wars and then cum back home to America and cant even git a JOB in this Muthafucka picking up PAPER cuz they done hired da white boy hoo ain't even got no HANDS to pick up da paper just cuz he White n Rite wit da Complection for Protection against Pauperism and fuck-a-nigga thats why wee shood never have stopped tryna separate frum the hate of the Barbarian hoo none is more Wicked than he is an Uncivilized Beast despite an abundance of Civilization wit no depth this is why we must pay attention to the ways of the white always without ASSUMING them as our own thus when a Crackkka wants to have a conversation bout the RACE problem their FRAGILITY never wants to hear shit bout Racism furthermore he is already Guilty in truth n spirit of his being so there is no reason to discuss wit White Folks about THEIR racist ways they already know meaning its stoopid to have a Black History Monf for example when if WHITEY doesnt know by now that Niggaz invented EVERYTHANG he will never know knowing this is a REVULSION of high merit to the Caucasoid mind hoo deep fears that the spirit of Niggaz will invade their psyche and make them U.S. even tho they WANNABE U.S. just the same they fight it on the surface yet git brown in the Sun as a form of reverse psychology of their insanity for they hate that our Nigganess is a Constant form of Identification that they have a love hate relationship wit they desire yet they Abhor it they know Niggaz are GODS and pray to us secretly in all Temples of Familiarity butt dont tell Us case we awaken to the Game of course Whitey will tell U he is an Atheist and does not bleeve in GOD or GODS then go in his basement and pray to a Black Mama or sum Nigga wit a long PHALLUS cuz they worship the Black Dick for which it is LIFE and LONGING why U think so many White men now love to see black men fucking their wives and girlfriends this is God Worship in the bedroom temples churches and other places of sacrality the black dick n pussy is boff loved and feared indeed the entire black body which was eaten by them STILL IS yet this is perverse worship they want the Nigga seed inside them to live as Us be us keep us wit em in their DNA n Spirit as it has always been this is the distinctive form that has to manifest in such a way as this to the white mind this is a love process in its most condensed shape manifestation source they want and need this foundation for their own spiritual expansion which fo niggaz dont include FAGS as Culture wich it can not be as much as they want it to be accepted as such behind all this is a basic castration attempt of the Nigga cuz a Nigga wit a Dick is considered Armed n Dangerous in the eyes of The Alabaster One **The longer I live it gits harder to**

separate REALITY frum FANTASY FACT frum FICTION and Mans MIND seems to be SLIPPIN into DARKNESS cuz that what Amerikkka wants mo than anythang is for a Nigga to be lost and turned out talkin PHILOSOPHY and FEELOSOPHY making Speeches so we Feel good we got a Piece butt No PEACE and what is a Piece butt sumpen frum a part of the WHOLE and hoo got the WHOLE PIE aint Niggaz we got the Whole CRY cuz dats all we do is Cry for PIE in da SKY while the GROUND is Stolen Rite Frum Under U.S. in the midst of WHITE NATIONALISM tom bout We All One United States sho long as its run by The White Man in the final analysis when Niggaz shood be sending Whitey to the Cemetery for Bury Gardens n let flowers spring up on his unkempt Grave that he bizzy putting US in via Diet n sanctioned Police Brutality ain't Anti-White Man Onliest Anti-The-White Mans oppression degradation exploitation sexploitation discrimination making BLACK a crime on any day of the week makes US Weak frum trickery treachery false promises let downs put downs stay down Clowns want us 2 B victims of day Corona Virus Americanism Racism Ism Jism Schemata caint stop this Nigga Nationalism doe Niggaz fighting for America and His Peeple still being done rong Nigga is a COP for America and Peeple dat look like him are still being done RONG and he or she dont give a fuck cuz they traded in their BLACK skin for a BLUE uniform so U kan see their Veins are Vain like their White Brothaz they done swore theirselves into as

True Blue that aint gone doo baby not even maybe not even close a billion miles away frum CLOSURE just plenty of Poseurs n Posers Supposing Suppositions feeding Niggaz more Superstitions frum da Position they occupy in da Hood up to No Good feted by STATEHOOD they werk n twerk for like Da Hoes they Are pulling Niggaz over in they CAR wont stop til its WAR then the BAR will be Reset n upset the Status Quo cuz like MALCOLM X said its War Crimes a ZOOMANITY against the Humanity of Black Peeple masquerading as SANITY and sum form of LAW found nowhere not even in Nature U just find OUR Blood running frum the TREES like Sap wee bee Saps give Uncle Sam DAP to continue fuckin wit him needa a NEW Road MAP and outta The White Mans VISE GRIP VICES Designer DISEASES wit no Ease Up in sight AIDS MADE 4 Niggaz in the Laboratories of The United States then shipped shaped into the Hoods Across Amerikkka including Tuberculosis Cancer strains as Main ingredients to be expedient engineering poverty too then say Niggaz are unemployable No Kan employ boy butt we doo enjoy taking yo Money wherever U may git it frum it cums back 2 us Crackkkaz as we kontinya to be da Jackkkaz of da Black Community thats cut off frum its Roots a FELLED nation in the Forest of Humanity hoo ain't made a sound as fell to the ground for our Black Lives to Matter thus our Niggaean Protests are always designed and destined to end in Repression and Misery and a distinguished footnote that will be taught to little ig-nant black boys n girls years later by Government Insurgents known as Teachers EARTH DAY is sponsored by MONSANTO The SUN is used to merely time when COVID-19 appears in a Niggaz Lungs Niggaz purpose must defy Logick in order to start being FREE Guerilla on Gorilla is the Rilla mooves we needa make for our sake n forsake all others hoo wood further stay in Lady Libertys pocket keep carrying a Torch 4 her of course the many-a-nigga hoo set themselves on for the Bitch is unprecedented in scope they also love the pedophile-loving pope no Joke its enuff to make U choke furthermo the Catholic Church got the world broke all yo parking speeding ticket fines go to make them stained glass windows fine all over the world they moove their Priest pedophiles to be safe butt not the children to be safe frum the Priests ya digg they offer the kids a swig of tha special juice they keep between their legs anno domini hail mary forgive me father NO forgive me child for continually raping U for the sake of The Church now bend over and dont tell Mommy wit Black Men its The Gubmint cuz we aint got to power wit our Black Wommins so we run to White Bitches hoo suck our DICKS frum the Rear wit a Tear they so happy to have the opportunity while the nappy-headed nigga bitch fights The Nigga all the days of her life dont wannabe his Wife just his Strife in fack it mite just be over forever tween the Nigga n Niggress cuz The White Man done got in the Black

Womans head n He Basikally OWNS the Pussy and her EBT card and College Degree that he paid for to send her to Skool wich always gone do before he send a basik Black Man merely to the Corner Sto plus Niggaz still divided on skin Color n Brand Name clothes they dam selves Thanks to Whitey aka Mr CHARLEY so the Average and I mean truly average Sista is only too happy to belong to a White Man even tho she came out the Nigga Nuts of her Pappy she wood not have even been a Girl wit good Pussy if it had notta been for a Black Man since the Nigga carries both Gene's to Make Girls and Boff Females or Males as the case may be thats an Ungrateful Hoe 4 U tho always forgitting where she came frum butt always wannabe Going where a Cracka tells her to report to and many-a-black man follows suit and disappears in the Albino cunt of the nearest white skank wit Thanks on his lipps Proud to dip his stick into the confines of her undeserving caves bitch juices then too watch the liberal white boy hoo offers U his shirt or access to success caint expect no less in a world in wich PUBLIC ENEMY is now PUBLICK ENEMIES #1 of each-um-other like the ghosts of Niggaz Past Member it was not UNCLE TOM butt SAMBO hoo was the real traitor to his Niggaz Uncle Tom was actually tryna HELP-A-Nigga out of so-called Slavery (seeing as how Niggaz whudden actually IN Enslaved in Amerikkka cuz thats just a popular Myth Amerikkka loves to feed n tell Niggaz to keep us feeling like inferior stock boys) so we kan keep putting up wif their shit on the shelf of the stores we shop and leave our money at which aint OUR stores butt the philosophy is the same NEGROIDS are SELL-OUTS of our own Mama Daddy Daughter Son Auntee Uncle Cousin to the Highest JEW Bidder and its always the JEWS wearing the SHOES wearing that ass out wit I have a dream speeches like they wrote for KING n sold to Negroes as Heroes troof was Zeroes Negoes fiddled smiled like Nero while King integrated U.S. into a Burning House butt we thought we gitting closer to the White House wif one of our peeples Whitey tole us to cum 2gether as a UNION butt dont forgit if its a UNION then its a GANG MAFIA see how they do U.S. thats hoo run the Economy GANGSTAZ called Politicians wif gang membas called Republicans Democrats Consituents Voters CRIME PAYS butt when they saw MALCOLM X whudden no Criminal and was taking they ass to World Court as WAR CRIMINALS they sent Negroids to Kill one of our own and blamed it on Real Niggaz same wif Martin Luther King when Malcolm shit start sinking into his Divine Nigga Attributes and wiping out his Negroism they sent one of THEIR own to shoot him frum the ground and blamed it on anutha white boy cross the way by da retarded name of JAMES EARL then annointed JESSE JACKSON as the heir near apparent since he was the most near n dear to Whitey that he wanted to succeed in a RAINBOW of Negroids funded by them see U kan never find a REAL NIGGA when U need one cuz most of em locked up anyway insteading accepting a payday ask GEORGE JACKSON he knows in his SOLE Niggaisdom what Im tom bout butt long as niggaz send happy songs lock arms wif white folks lives hoo live at black lives matter concerts in a concerted effort blood will continue to flow as niggaz git aborted by Lady Liberty hoo dont wear no draws n never intended to have niggaz cumming outta her in the first place then Crackkkaz got the nerve to be mad that Niggaz make to much noise when we die when the last breathe leave our chestses niggaz still dying fist first in the air tryna overcum 400 years of civil rites incites took like a thief in the nite by our plight now we own the GHETTOES sold to us by JEWS after they had them first then left em for cleaner Dollars in the suburbs but loving the Dirty Dollar Niggaz pay em for the trap cracked houses we live in Illuminati un-illumined by proper lite unenlightened consciousness butt if a Nigga hit that 4321 STRAIGHT instead of BOX will he WAKE UP to the GAme thats being plate outcheah or will he moove out Da Hood like we all doo when we doo better and dont have to receive no mo letters from certain kinds of peeples hoo werk for the Gubmint Authorities butt kno this there be such a niggaz waiting like Richard Pryor said on the hunting grounds of hoods for that moment to hatch in a Nigga memory and we gone be the Last Revolutionaries just-a-walkin in the Sun rite now tho niggaz caint afford to be Niggaz Huemans that shit cost and they caint aint paying U.S. enuff to bluff our way throo like we do them tests they give us to test our IQ shid I QUIT so quit tryna Reason wif Racists hoo have no Reason to be alive let-a-lone Reasoning they married U.S. to Amerikkka and didnt even ask if we wanted to be Fucked by her low standards so we sang Negro Standards OIL & GAS started by a Rockefeller fella hoo hate black folks that he take Oil frum in Afrika tho after he pump in the ass for blood diamonds he sell at the pump see how they doo U.S.at all times of the nite and day white men are Brutes by instinct not intellect ya digg whereas this is why no discussions or conclusions kan be reached in a diplomatic manner wif a gentlemans agreement when aint no gentle men present before during after there aint no nurture for this type-a-nature mah nigga increase and progress is lost here only ignorance abounds like weeds in a garden that has long since passed due to destruction rudeness lewdness lasciviousness their roots are torn up obliterated the womb that birthed them destroyed and aint convenient in these parts no mo if it ever was and it whudden im giving U strate valid testimony flat out confession the goal of our enemies is to keep us without perfect peace in despair of perpetual darkness cuz NIggaz git tricked n shit into believing dollars n dogmas go 2gether when they dont wont caint wind up consenting to a lie upon lie upon anutha lie rather than free will whereas sum Negroids think that means VOTING having the Right To Vote is like having the RIGHT To REMAIN SILENT and U know why U have the Right To Remain cuz U under arrest Foo Crackkkaz said they gave Niggaz Right and aint acted right since meanwhile how U gone be given sumpen U were Born wit yo rights aint left cuz they left long time ago soon as they were give to U yet this was the FRUIT they give to Niggaz frum a Poisonous Tree no less Therefore the world of White Gaze shood never be amazed when Niggaz turn down their offers cuz of lost patience distrust them wanting us to be FAke Niggaz when we Real Niggaz wit a head for avoiding their transitory seduction delusion n collusion and calling it love for Our Peeple this is why Erry Nigga erry REAL nigga is a Doubting Thomas n Every Thang MUST be Doubted of the White Man of our historical dealings and he must be removed frum the Ballot n Ballad of our lives Such NEW NIggaz are here and not just hangin on the horizon ready to commit heretical acts of dismemberment that cleave n slice Us away frum HIM under proper heredity thereby Im imploring YOU, U and especially You and YOU kno hoo U are to negate heretofore what All Niggaz have been cumming up under and dealing wit as an Un-truth white men have been our IDOLS for far too long and we must now Cross-Examine All Idols which are nothing butt Intellectual Fallacies anyhow (Tribal Cave-Mind Marketplace Free Market Bizness Commerce Theater Sports Games Bullshit) that we indulge in constantly to our detriment money spent behind on rent waiting to be rescued by Clark Kent Superman White Man THE MAN cuz we fell for their shit when they built castles in the sky for US hoes and them Pimps Pimpin is what they doo on the real deal NOT the ideal thats just more IDOLS we never question until now we better sludge hammer to ALL the Nigga werk has only just begun on that inflated shit if we wannabe free living as Gods or living as Animals of the lowest order For a Man must take a chance on being a Man he only gits once chance and he gotta take that chance if he gone fight for what he bleeve for much as Niggaz been done rong he gotta take that chance even if it kill him even if it putt him down in the ground Niggaz gotta git they gun dont run nowhere to go but to even the score thats what the AUTHENTIC Ones within US must doo instead of thinking we gaining High Favor because we Obeying Instruction Accepting Reproof without Proof are Troof wich by now so many of US kno not of or even WHERE it be foe Truth is long gone Missing frum Niggaz we made truth an ORPHAN abandoned it to THEM to raise it up as they saw fit except it aint Fit for shit butt exists in the Pulpit in the Moufs of Our Turncoats Snitches n Traitors Haters Prevaricators hoo been Promised they were to Be made Dictators of U.S. and this they have loved above all especially their Own without Morals without Honor without Loyalty only to the Ones hoo SAID they were HEROES of the THRONE and their HEIRS hoo are Not Nuthing butt TALES frum at least TWO Cities that were

Symptoms of their history that plainly tells U they were nuthing butt VAGABINDS URCHINS Homeless Widows Drunkards Theives Rapists MurderersNOT Kings which is to say NIGGAZ for dats what NIGGA means KING NIGKS NICKS NIKKAS ST SNICK Saint Nickolaus Saint Nigga Claus wich is BLACK for Charcoal these Enemies of Wee The Peeple never had Morals or Morality or MOORality Black Authenticity never ever had even a TRADITION of Morality its not a werd that exists among CAVE MEN yadigg its description defies categorization among such Peeple hoo only a stolen mystery history always laying claim to WHAT aint theirs based on a MYTH they wrote and said GOD that they Sold the world butt especially Niggaz Tole em to name it claim it and it wood be so according to ordained pape werk forged underground in a laboratory mountain in Israel not on ancient maps nowhere butt in feaux fake illustrated drawn Jew then baked the forgery in an oven so the writing wood stick and have that fresh out the OVEN smell to it and 6 Million testimonial lies signed in declaration to das boot they gave it to Calhoun Tubbs to write a sing bout it butt he wouldnt cuz he cood tell it wasnt no TRUE BLUES story it was ripped off Intellectual Property of Niggaz including our thoughts insights breath sinew essence blood bones tears sweat spit spittle our Whatever Forever & a day thru pure Vileness Bileness and Feces attitude all part of the plan using diabolikal Nigga Psychology yet its all based on Crackkka Inferiority see butt what they do is package the shit up in breadcrumbs and offer it for sale to starving nigga on Slick Avenue and what unfufilled negro wouldnt buy it since its the only thang betwee him her and NUTHING butt Allah or God hoo wont dont stop Whitey frum Blowing Up Mosques n Churches wit Niggaz in em only protect Synagogues of Satan where Jews hang out wailing on a wall in Kufi Kaps wit secrets in em cuz GOD werk for them sabbath days or as needed basis they own the SKY that HEAVEN is in thru the FAA and if God rejects their offer they pull their Sponsorship and threaten him wit having to answer prayers in the hoods for the rest of his life and he dont want that shit read 100 THINGS ABOUT The RACIST WHITE TRASH CRACKKKA WITH CUMPLETE PROOF by JA ROGERS its all in there DONALD TRUMP is Chapter 2 hoo became the prophecy fulfilled the dismemberment of peeple commercialization of black lives immaterial its always the same problem reaction solution got most Niggaz not wanting REVENGE just Relief and willing to obtain by spitting in each other eye throw shade n dust to defile one anutha frum any form of nobility respectability later for each according to his ability or needs our dreams are fat butt our reality is slim chances to none we niggaz are legends living among fires of hatred we caint putt out cuz our worldly passions have been stoked to burn as eternal internal flame yet we run these hoods while wee run around IN these hoods our baselessness growing as flowers frum the concrete talkin bout hard times in a rap song that has boundless potential to rise up the chart stream so we think true Emancipation is a social media account wit a multitude of followers n viral neuroses screamed for 2 minutes looking into a selfie camera since its hard to rebuke ones self aggrandizement or point out imperfections butt kan we blame everythang on The Albino Ones mostly yes they hold out the knife wit the honey of fame wealth money and Niggaz lick it cut themselves deep n drank the blood n die happy of the sweet wound they are those content to be conquered butt just like the Good Holy Book of Niggmaste tells us that iron sharpens iron and sharp nigga sharpens sharp nigga except most of us have dullards full of rust thus nothing kan grow predominately frum us only impure sincerity so what kan we expect the real state of thangs to bee beehind this butt more causes conditions attritions without distinctions to infinity n beeyond quantity this urges ever the more that Niggaz need independent isolation to go wit the independent origination cuz our integration is the source of Niggaz grieving lamenting crying dying in pain agony n infamy since frum the beginning our relationship wit whitey has been only Calamities unavoidable ignorance restlessness and mental blindness and never a true Fack about the bearing of Desire upon our Huemanity so we have been dislodged frum how to ride n glide and maneuver in this world we have no longer a konnection to the true reason for the erection of shit

Niggaz be gitting born in a pure state then becum talked into being carriers of suffrage as salvation that shit becums our vow and wee devotees burning incense candles to gods that dont exist when carrying worshipping a god is merely a hindrance baggage for a journey of a thousand miles that shood be a single step show and proove keep in mind that Whitey is highly koncerned that if Niggaz whose blood is in essence without malignancies n fallacies wakes up n break thru into true mental freedom he will be killed by U.S. so Amerikkka SHE stay ready and ever on guard that Niggaz thoughts stay stuck on Stoopid Distraction so we never git no Traction or Perform Action only exhibit Reactions that wood make the White Trash Hegels Wagner Marxs Engels proud that his plans continue to werk nearly 200 years later so Niggaz bear watching at all times unless we becum emancipated enlightened REALIZED NIGGAZ practicing and disciplined in THE WAY OF THE NIGGA a supremely insightful ONE hoo has attained NIGGAHOOD in the midst of the conflagration enveloping the world for the Enemy does not want The Nigga to cultivate such a diligent self respeck aspeck of the REAL NIGGA NATURE like this that wood moove U.S. out of Self Delusion especially of right words thinking the right werds to the rong muthafuckaz such as the Enemy wich is pearls before swine fragrance to a funky flower right teaching to the rong student makes for a long ass class where the bell never rings to end it and too often this is Niggaz hoo becum Whiteys Magical Negro then soon as we show him how its done wee became his White Mans Burden while he becums a Niggaz Grief Amerikka will never be able to understand ALL dat Niggaz carry within them the seeds for building a world lay within the Divine Nigga Attributes DNA of darker blooded ones memory instinct girded by impossible to fathom knowing rests in U.S. always exploited sexploited for greed gain for the white world knows not what to do wit U.S. Niggaz except trample Us under their Teachings embedded in fear bondage oriented likings e-vil what we kan do hoo kan be what we are capable of goes wasted cuz Amerikkka cant remove her resentment to contentment her heathenry dominates gives impunity to false ideas allows the peeple hoo trust her ignorantly to be crushed into powder there was a time being Homeless in society meant One of Divinity Sustenance Wizdom now it means Downtrodden forsaken puttdown frum a Beatdown by the Country S/He worships in denial of its evilness power monopolies lies over truth protected by a circle of lies We niggaz the many the few continue to love Whitey long after he never loved U.S. thus we keep looking back upon a mythical picture that was painted thru hypocritical palettes oaths of sumpen that never meant to be sumpen that we THOUGHT it was we live off that for we are dumb asses in that respeck while we wait for the DEVIL to Cum for Whitey we fail to realize He IS the Devil hoo has already cum but not for Himself but for U.S. when we ask why S/He uses one explanation to explain anutha explanation and apparently we never hear the answer and dont hang round for it either we are unwhole in that way butt Imma tell U sumpen we living in the last days of Crackerdom-ination where they git to act like Doms and keep Niggaz as Bottoms politcal bedfellows cuz this revelation baby babylon falling like dominoes n old hoes out on their last stroll round the block for cock diggin the scene reckless eyeballing for a dollar they kan snatch frum a Trick meanwhile roaches running outta the crack of her Albino cunt cuz the lights cumming on in the Dicks of Niggaz katching Awakening taking note of the Coat-Tail Pulling at last thats long been tryna inform the Skulls of U.S. of the play so we wouldnt stay Lames Simps our naive minds is cumming out da gutter peeping the fallacious fraud of Whiteys folklore shit like going to the Moon in Cancer and became cancerous to the entire world while at the same time denying dat Niggaz are frum MARS when they dont know GREECE frum GREASE fo real WEE waking up out dat SLUMBER they wrote the story GULLIVER bout them little bitty muthafuckaz was the White Specks of Huemanity that had Gulliver The Giant Nigga tied down we broke the ropes tho he tryna still be MOBY DICK cuz when ya peep all his fairy tales novels n whatnot he constantly showing U how he WANNA do it or GONE do it to The World especially where ever Niggaz Is at and Where aint

Niggaz not at a BLACK RUSSIAN is real shit ya unnerstandme Niggaz may be a cliche cuz wee SALT of the Earth but the Ancestors dont like UGLY on U.S. like dat there and seeing the Destruction of a Peeple built rite outta da Soil they done became a part of so they done ARMED us Niggaz left behind so we wont be totally destroyed frum The Enemy feeding upon our Skins in Melanated Weight on the open market Niggaz is going back to knowing shit 1,000 years before Whitey gits wind of it befo him even born WEE going back to storing Knowingness in our fingertips and the whole world in our hands gone keep a song in our heart a glide in our stride a dip in our hip and the rite magickal phrases on our lips **Mo Niggaz are being CALLED and Mo Niggaz are being CHOSEN to do this werk of comission** bout to go to the 4 corners of the world and universe too and it aint gone git quiet til er body done heard this shit this new drop of slop *The Holy Book of Niggamaste tells us that NUTHING KAN STOP A NIGGA WHOSE TIME HAS CUM* as Niggaz gain cognizance we aint nobdys assets or ass and so it is and mote it be Black Peeple like US is cumming out the White Mans BOOKS ready to inhabit our own age of endless victory rather than non-stop victimization in the new kingdom niggadom time to be posted up as countless ageless unparalleled power emanating frum niggaz pores cuz aint no Answers in they books dam sho taint no Solutions how kan it be when they dont actually kno The QUESTIONS anyway the BOOK is in a Nigga chapter verse page number contents n index authored by the Niggods inside who werk off the childhood principle of IM RUBBER YOU GLUE WHATEVER U SAY TO ME BOUNCES OFF OF ME and STICKS TO YOU and it does Whitey got KARMA cumming thats worse than Retaliation Radiation see cuz You got KaRMA and thens U got PAYBACK now Karma is a BITCH butt Payback is a MUTHAFUCKA for those hoo done sought Niggaz out for pure oppression suppression depression just all the Pression possible the plantation is now the corporation yeah wee know that shit now thats why for the New Real Nigga the VOTE is now the RE-VOLT out these Nigga moufs Prayer is obsolete mute wrapped up spit out useless denounced sent back frum whence it came FINISHED amen selah gone way frum heah wit dat shit DONE fuck dat Protest Mess too walking in anutha Nigga shoes like that dont FIT the action necessary no mo Fuck dat Sangin WEE Swangin now no Praying Wee SLAYING now Im SAYING Niggaz gotta leave the Cracka and his world of IDEAS behind and keep OUR feetses on the Ground GROUNDED not that Ideas aint bout that butt that soon they be a BOOK of ACCEPTED IDEAS that shoulda been Rejected Not Respected instead wee bee carrying the joint round reading n absorbing nonsensical parabolic permutated mutated parables all that its bout that aint got a god-dam thang to do wit Nigga Folk in the main a Perversion of high order to fall for this Perception which then becums the principle of sufficient reason we base U.S. knowing on in other werds now we kno nothing but what we been tole to know by those hoo themselves dont know See we dem Niggaz hoo done changed the warmth of our Blood for Generations tossed out the Habits blemishes of a bygone Race into their Face **cuz Nigga like mahself aint gone rest** cuz we Inconsolable see the betrayal by Enemies n Frenemies time for them to be Served Up treachery is a book we must write ourselves this day aware now that Cowardness is hard to cure wee act Spinning wizdom on its head wee see now in a different way what must be done understand that a RIVER is still a ROAD yadigg a road that mooves n grooves know when its time to burn out mah Niggaz different seasons brang different Diseases feelme No longer slaves to the riddim tricks or Johns except the HIgh Conquering One wee tapped into n useta didnt know it now we do we got dat majick baby all our Humiliations bout to be sped out ate up devoured bout to roll off us like flop sweaty sex butt U.S. Real Niggaz done broke up wit whiteys tenets cuz 2+2=FIVE in their world U aint kno now U kno they all instinct No Intuition which they killed wit Empicism in the Age of Enlightenment that was Dark Ages fo real wich proceeded to cum out of them like hemorrhoids like low hangin fruit Niggaz kno better now than to trust anybody that would blame a woman for fucking up apples trees then start hangin Niggaz frum em as strange fruit ripe for the picknicking or send Niggaz to die for poppy seeds and if they dont turn em into heroin addicts or lovers of Fetanyl so they kan die wit Prince Michael Jackson after being framed wit James Brown n Michael Jordan daddy then say Robin Williams killed em all wit Jokes he was shooting up wit Richard Pryor n Ray Charles JACK that aint Homeostasis Homies its time to protect yo Third EYE and I The Will to I AM is written to be exercised stricken against the heads Amerikkka hoo will never change in their pure impulsive Urge in how they see Niggaz so we must never change in how we will fuck them up irrepressibly irresponsibly irresistably irregardlessly cuz there is No reasoning wit Whitey always bent on dictatorship as the most common method of Governing against becumming always ready to use a gun when a hammer will doo always ready to Annihilate rather than meditate butt Niggaz I implore U 2 memba that yo thoughts are the speed of light which is already in the past when it hits earth so are YOU and YOURS the things we are thinking of now We actually thought bout 1,000 years ago befo we got here as stationary earthlings on immoveable earth in the future we now live as all thangs are Present the Past WAS and the Future IS the cumplete arrangement of the Cosmos is reflected in You thus we know TIME was automatically created IN you when all Niggaz came 2gether in a Primordial Orgasm slide thru the portal at the same time we got heah as **Part King Part God Mostly NIGGA so the MOMENT is NOW is the time for all Real Niggaz to cum to the Aid of ALL**

real niggaz in this country and those hoo wONt or CanT it wood have been betta they had not been born to have stayed out of hueman form hopefully they will expire dry up as dog shit for we need them not for the Rebirth of Tragedy U.S. Niggaz of the moment are bout the Audacity of NOPE Hope is Biblical this shit now is CYCLICAL Timing and the Immoralists time to be Dead has arrived as a cool breeze upon our faces and cold water upon our Thirst to walk as truly Liberated Men on Earth WEE must Proceed and THEY must Recede as so many Epidemics of WHITENESS must by Violence where necessary let yo MOUFS utter the werds NO MORE as Initiatory Act of REVULSION and Revolution as a first step to Destroying The MONSTER that is Neanderthal White Human hoo had the first evil thawt upon earth not merely a physical destruction or even ONLY that but the Monster Frankenstein that S/He is and wishes to insert that Innergy into US and has on many Niggaz we are LIKE them in erry way for the White Mans philosophy is strictly based on a WILL TO LIVE to POWER to DISCHARGE that Power and Impose His Will on Niggaz its not OUR way its his way not the NIGGA WAY or the WAY of the NIGGA this is his Superfluous Principles at work running on Instinct that tells him to KILL all and Preserve Himself SELF-PRESERVATION and Yo ANNIHILATION via whatever method necessary Maslows hierarchy of needs is REVERSED wit the Alabaster Disaster waiting to happen in other werds he will be

SPIRITUAL if that is to happen only AFTER he wipes Niggaz off the face of the Earth whereas Niggaz are Spiritual FIrst only see WAR as a last refuge of a Desperate Plea by a muthafucka that he dont wanna HURT U wee like the HULK in that way dont make NIGGAZ Angry cuz U wont like U.S. when we git Angry wich is well within OUR right rites to so n be so when we plainly see that Crackkkaz have been Improvising the werld ORDER in their Image only n teaching it as Gospel Tenets and it be Niggaz fault fo our Error in not Knowing The Skriptures of True Prophecy or in going Wayard frum da Muthafuckaz and losing our Advantage as well as Our NIGGA WAY and WAYS becoming thus Imprisoned in Whiteys Wet Dream instead of being that Unsettling force to Whiteys Establishment in repast we have known this butt have not Acted Upon such reasonable Rite insite they have made Niggaz distrust their senses into seeing only our Lying Eyes resulting in Weak judgement lack of experiment when at one time we knew how to bridge the two of Science n sense knowing overall that a Nigga COMMONSENSES Is GREATER Than PSCIENCE denial of this caused Our Decay and Withering frum heights butt at this point in the Game Real Niggaz among U.S. have awakened n arisen months FACK dat TRUTH is Our Province and the Sovereign Nature of Hueman Gods Niggods as we ARE n still becoming as we un-cum from the hum of the CON we fell for and git back into the LIGHT of SENSE and The Light of REASON the Wrecking Ball of Nigga Gnosis be our Freedom our Illumined Black Sabbath **frum being Tortured Bones to SALVATION Nation In da NEW NIGGADOM WORLD ORDER** The Dirt in da Hoods have Shifted they have Shitted in the Streets long enuff 4 U.S. to know I'm in niggaz Psychic shit now I want Yo mind Butter n Toast so smoove wee long been held Inferior for Ulterior Motive nuthing devotive bout it except wee been Devoted to the singular cause of helping brang harm to our own Self The Sands have SHIFTED wit Niggaz Consciousness yadigg so dat the Ante is Up Interplanetary assistance is now running wit-a-Nigga Heads have stopped OBEYING so THEY gotta LIVE n take dat shit sumwhere else See WHITEY tryna git off Earth dont U well thats cuz of U.S. having eyes dats cum open as newly borned instead of being Burned by them Foos erry where in space Whitey go he Trespassing without a Passport long as he gone tho sneaking to hit off this Muthafucka when he think Niggaz ain't looking BYE wee dont give a fuck like dat The WERDS of Niggaz Past have cum back to HAUNT HONKIES & HELP Niggaz as it was and IS written that they be Smitten Smited Wiped out so EARTH aka New Jerusalem cood be clean there is a reason white is the Color that gits Dirtyest the fastest see genetic footnotes that explains the Aberrations are embedded and such Peeple have no choice butt 2 B hoo wee see they are and have becum 1nce they came frum Underground replete wit dat R-Complex intact on the attack stretching the Innocent Pope I saw em on a Rack back to back its the dawn of a Nu Day thats been on it's way since fo ever n a day as they say where wee cum frum Niggaz may have been caught between 2 Stools and been the Footstool of an odd Evil God butt no longer that hunger baby the Nigga Soul is Nuthing to do wit Double Consciousness every Thang to do wit aching to Express itself Conscientiously Expeditiously Expialidociously WEE now be those hoo have woke up to having acquired the rong racial knowledge Influence yadigg cuz wee took a swigg off the erroneous fountain of Goof defiling our natyal expression making it flee us n wee not bee all wee cood bee got swooned n CONNED by gentle talk later stalked by severe strikes n conquers dat have not passed quickly as wee kan clearly see 2020 is still 1920 wit invented man made laboratory plague diseases revisiting itself upon Us Frum those grecian minds of british invention of an always known inferior race came the DECEPTION wich bee their revolt against the Fathers of them wich be U.S. they arose out between the caves walls they Scratched on like werewolves to plunder devour Niggaz hoo cood not be wholly killed they were the Crackkkaz hoo had landed gentry in their imaginations when they were but poverty scum n scorched earth fast forwarded to the **same old same old courtesy of Mike Browns same old same old Breonna Taylors same old same old George Floyds same old same old Sandra Bland same old same old EMMETT TILL the SAME OLD SAME OLD** so u see mah Niggaz the buck dancing stops here along wit da fear i swear fo god cross mah heart hope they die so how we gone cum up rev how we gone do it how we gone take back whats rightfully fundamentally basikally all ours when we aint got no bullets bombs weapons or factory ownership to create propaganda to fuck they minds uppeth i see the questions on yo faces bout how we gone artfully dodge this shit its an art to this war so several of our lives will be used to ruin their strength butt we will command nature use worms to eat their crops starved bellies give in resolve fades desire leaves a muthafucka when the body is weak spells catch a fools heart when they dont kno how to prepare against it thats why Marcus Garvey said use the whirl winds mah Niggaz whitey mo superstitious than niggaz on the real peep their myths n they scatter like leaves in a whirl wind all this is in order when we face the cumplete truth we a race apart and gotta giving being one wit them that shit is dead as old men wit one foot in the grave living wit parasites as relatives naked I came in blood returning the same in pussy before that doe we have arrived at understanding niggaz is at dat place where we kan use supernatural talents abilities gifts skills imaginations sending the enemy back under the soil frum whence he came that is our obligation legacy to stop singin and start swingin release our addictions to caucasion persuasion wit prejudice n revulsion in our hearts until the bell tolls and we back on top OR least where we sposed **2 B this is the summoning to return to the way of nigga folk back to the nigga way**

Contact: reverendniggadaddy@yahoo.com

Subscribe: www.patreon.com/reverendniggadaddy

SocialMedia:
www.instagram.com/reverendniggadaddy

Bookings & Workshops: 314-875-0482

www.ingramcontent.com/pod-product-compliance
Lightning Source LLC
Chambersburg PA
CBHW072100290426
44110CB00014B/1760